THE
COMING ONE

THE
COMING ONE

A. B. Simpson

WHITAKER
HOUSE

Publisher's note: This new edition from Whitaker House has been updated for the modern reader. Some words, expressions, sentence structure, and punctuation have been revised for clarity, readability, and accuracy. In addition, a number of biblical references have been added to indicate exact quotation of Scripture or allusions to Scripture.

Unless otherwise indicated, all Scripture quotations are taken from the King James Version of the Holy Bible. Scripture quotations marked (NKJV) are taken from the *New King James Version*, © 1979, 1980, 1982, 1984 by Thomas Nelson, Inc. Used by permission. All rights reserved. Scripture quotations marked (YLT) are taken from *Young's Literal Translation of the Bible* (1898) by Robert Young. The material in the italicized brackets was included by Young; the material in Roman brackets was added for clarity.

Boldface type in the Scripture quotations indicates the author's emphasis.

The Coming One:
What Scripture Teaches About the End Times

ISBN: 978-1-62911-187-2
eBook ISBN: 978-1-62911-188-9
Printed in the United States of America
© 2014 by Whitaker House

Whitaker House
1030 Hunt Valley Circle
New Kensington, PA 15068
www.whitakerhouse.com

Library of Congress Cataloging-in-Publication Data (Pending)

1 2 3 4 5 6 7 8 9 10 11 12 ⨄ 22 21 20 19 18 17 16 15 14

NOTE FROM THE PUBLISHER

While Whitaker House does not necessarily agree with all the eschatological conclusions of A. B. Simpson (1843–1919), we did not want to offer a book that "cleaned up" the author's ideas for the contemporary reader. Simpson's teachings reflect certain branches of thought in the array of Christian thinking and interpretation of the end times throughout the centuries. We feel that *The Coming One* has a place in the body of Christian literature concerning the second coming of Jesus Christ, and that its contents are useful for an overall study of end-times themes, as well as for understanding the necessity of personal preparation for Christ's return.

CONTENTS

CHAPTER ONE

THE POINT OF VIEW

"Grace be unto you, and peace, from him which is, and which was, and which is to come [the coming One]."
—Revelation 1:4

Did the Lord Jesus Christ complete His work on earth during His first advent and leave to secondary agents and spiritual influences the finishing of His great plan of redemption? Or, did He simply accomplish the first stage of that great work, and is He coming back again in person to this old earth someday to complete that glorious plan? These questions, in short, summarize what has passed into theological discussion as the postmillennial versus the premillennial view of the second advent, or coming, of the Lord.[1]

Inadequate Arguments Against the Premillennial View

In the first place, let us look at the objections that are made by many to the doctrine of the premillennial coming of the

Lord Jesus. Then, we will turn to the positive side—the case for premillennialism.

Christ's Coming Is Fulfilled at the Death of His Saints

There are some who believe that the promises of Christ's coming are all fulfilled in the death of His saints—that, at death, the coming of the Lord is realized, in practical terms, by each one of us individually. It is enough to say that there is the widest contrast between death and the Lord's coming—rightly understood. Death separates us from our friends; the Lord's coming reunites us with our friends. Death brings us to be with the Lord; the Lord's coming brings the Lord to be with us. Death is the curse of sin; the Lord's coming cancels the curse forevermore.

Perhaps a single passage in the New Testament is a sufficient inspired proof that, in the mind of Christ and the Holy Spirit, these are wholly diverse, and the one cannot be the fulfillment of the other. In speaking to Peter (and John) before His ascension, the Lord told Peter by what death he would die. The evangelist interpreted His words to Peter as *"signifying by what death he should glorify God"* (John 21:19). Immediately afterward, Jesus said about John, *"If I will that he tarry till I come, what is that to thee?...Then went this saying abroad among the brethren that that disciple should not die"* (John 21:22–23). This clearly shows that the coming of Christ is the very opposite of dying. The phrase *"tarry till I come"* implied that perhaps John would not die at all. The idea of comparing death with the Lord's coming is wholly contrary to the thought that was in the mind of the Lord.

In speaking to the Thessalonians about their friends who had passed on, the apostle Paul did not comfort them by saying, "You ought to be very glad, because the Lord has come for them." On the contrary, he said, "You ought to be comforted, because some day the Lord is coming for them." (See 1 Thessalonians 4:13–18.) Surely, this is scarcely worth an argument. The Lord meant something very much more than death when He spoke of His return.

Christ's Coming Was Fulfilled at the Destruction of Jerusalem

Some people apply Christ's coming to the destruction of Jerusalem, which occurred in the year AD 70, shortly after the Lord's ascension. Now, it would seem very strange to a patriotic Jew to be told that the thing that was to him the brightest and sweetest hope of his holy faith [the coming of the Messiah in kingly reign] actually meant a tragedy of fire and blood that was to destroy the city and the temple that he loved and plunge millions of his race into temporal and eternal ruin. To call that the coming of the Lord and the fulfillment of the blessed hope (see Titus 2:13) would surely be a travesty on all consistent thought and all common sense. If no other reason were available, it is enough to say that the destruction of Jerusalem occurred a quarter of a century before the book of Revelation was written, and the one theme of that book, from first to last, is *"Behold, I come"* (Revelation 3:11; 16:15; 22:7, 12).

Christ's Coming Refers to His Spiritual Indwelling

There are many who apply the Lord's coming to His personal visitation to the hearts of His people. Jesus said, *"I will not leave you orphans; I will come to you"* (John 14:18 NKJV), and *"We [the Father and Jesus] will come unto him, and make our abode with him"* (John 14:23). I have heard people say, "Oh, it is all very well for you to talk about the Lord's coming, but He has already come to us, and we are satisfied." I wonder if He came to these people any more intimately than He came to John the Beloved! I wonder if John did not have the Lord in his heart as deeply and delightfully as the most advanced modern saints! Yet, it was John who said, *"When he shall appear, we shall be like him; for we shall see him as he is. And every man that hath this hope in him purifieth himself, even as he is pure"* (1 John 3:2–3). Have these "advanced saints" gotten closer to Christ than Paul did? Yet, it was Paul who said, *"We...shall be caught up...to meet the Lord in the air: and so shall we ever be with the Lord"* (1 Thessalonians 4:17). The truth is, the more intimately we have Christ in our hearts, the more ardently we will long for His personal and visible return, for Christ in us is *"the hope of glory"* (Colossians 1:27).

Christ's Coming Is a "Millennium of Principles and Progress"

Others apply the promise of the Lord's coming to the spreading of the gospel and to the influence of the truth through the church in all the world, bringing about a millennium of principles and spiritual progress. This, they tell us, is the true millennium and the real coming of the Lord; and some of them think that through the progress of modern civilization, it is already nearly here, if it has not already come. Surely, that was not the Lord's idea. He told us that when He comes, instead of there being men and women longing to welcome Him and to bow at His feet in worship and service, there will scarcely be *"faith on the earth"* (Luke 18:8). And He said, *"And as it was in the days of* [Noah], *so shall it be also in the days of the Son of man* [when the Son of Man will be revealed] (Luke 17:26). They will be busy about everything else but Him. They will be finding their delight in everything else but in the prospect of His coming and His reign.

We do not have space to trace the vision of the Master as He tells us what the future of the church is to be before His return. But, certainly, it is anything but a millennium. Nor do we find much sign of a millennium in even our best Christian lands. The reports of the progress of Christianity tell of declining membership, declining contributions for missions, and declining faith on the part of the church. The world will not be watching for Him, but *"as a snare shall it come on all them that dwell on the face of the whole earth"* (Luke 21:35). It will not be the climax of human progress, but it will be the catastrophe of all earthly pride.

Christ's Coming Is to Be Interpreted Spiritually

There are many who tell us that the prophecies of the Old Testament have a special spiritual meaning, and that they refer to His inward reign in the hearts of Christians and through the principles of the gospel in human society. There is a spiritualizing tendency that would blot out the literal Israel from the future history of the world and appropriate all the promises Christ gave to the Israelites for ourselves. Do not wonder, therefore, that Israel has turned the tables upon us and has spiritualized all that the Old Testament prophets said about the first coming of Christ.

A section of the church is spiritualizing all that the Old Testament said about the coming King, and Israel is spiritualizing all that the Bible has said about the Lamb of God. The latter takes the fifty-third chapter of Isaiah to mean the suffering nation of Israel, and it is just as much justified in this as modern theological teachers are when they explain away the promises of Christ's glorious reign as mere spiritual imagery.

A Premillennial Coming Would Mean That God Had "Failed"

Again, they tell us it would be a great dishonor to the Holy Spirit to say that He was not adequate for the complete regeneration of human society—that if God does not, through the present agencies in the church and the world, completely defeat the power of evil and make all things new, the Holy Spirit has failed, and God has not been equal to the task of saving humanity. Perhaps that is the strongest argument that the postmillennialists use. They say, "We believe God is equal to the task, and before the gospel has finished its work, it is going to close every saloon, save every sinner, and make every desert to blossom as the rose."

At first sight, there is a good deal in this argument that is plausible. But, if you think for a moment, you will agree that if that was God's plan—if it was God's intention to take all evil out of the world in the present age; if it was God's intention to make everything pure, good, and holy now—He has made an awful failure of it. We should be ashamed of the gospel if that is the best that it can do. The awful conditions of human society today would be a frightful travesty of divine power and grace, if that was all God meant to do. Therefore, our answer is this: God never meant to do this and never said He would. God said He was going to gather out of the nations *"a people for his name"* (Acts 15:14), and the world would go on as it had gone on, and "the wicked would still do wickedly, and none of the wicked would understand" (see Daniel 12:10).

When we thus understand His plan, we will not be discouraged; but we are in utter despair if we do not so understand it. Dr. Kellogg said that the first years of his life in India would have broken his heart due to the awful sway of heathenism and wickedness—and the scant rays of gospel light after all that had been done—were it not for the hope of Christ's coming. Thank God He has not failed, and some glorious day we will fully understand.

A Millennial Reign Is too Material for Spiritual Minds

Some tell us that this doctrine of the Lord's return and the setting up of a glorious terrestrial millennium is too material, earthly, and sensuous for spiritual minds—that all these things are figures, and God is lifting our hearts and hopes to something more spiritual and less earthly. They say that in this present "childhood" age, we are dealing with the physical and visible, but we are going to pass on to a higher realm where all will be purely spiritual.

That is the greatest heresy of the present day. It began with spiritualizing the story of creation, and the result was the modern doctrine of Darwinian evolution. The idea that Genesis is but an allegory was the beginning, and Christian Science is the climax, with its basic principle that there never was anything created, and that everything is unreal. That is where false spiritualizing takes you.

The Liberal Theology goes further and says that Jesus was an "idea" and that there was no historical Christ, no cross, and no resurrection; it was all an idea in the minds of mystics. If He did ever live and die, His dust is still sleeping under the Syrian stars. That is what spiritualizing does. It takes out of God's Book all reality, making everything merely a dream as vague as the fooleries of Christian Science. Thank God that He is real, and that we are real, and that Christ is real, and that the coming glory is real, and that *"this same Jesus…shall so come* [again] *in like manner as ye have seen him go into heaven"* (Acts 1:11).

The Premillennial Point of View

Is there positive proof that we may look for a premillennial coming of the Lord?

Christ Came to Earth Previously

The Lord has been here already; the Lord Jesus lived on this globe of ours literally—actually treading its material surface with His holy feet and saturating its soil with His precious blood. He has been a citizen of this earth. Why should it be thought something incredible that He should come back again to His old home? If He actually lived here once, why should He not actually come here again?

How simple that is! Here He once initiated His work. Why should He not come back and finish it? Here He once fought the battle. Why should He not come back and wear the crown of victory and *"see of the travail of his soul, and...be satisfied"* (Isaiah 53:11)? Here He once paid the fearful price. Why should He not come back to win the great reward? That is what He Himself said. He is like "a nobleman going to a far country to receive for himself a kingdom and then return." (See Luke 19:12.) There is nothing transcendent or novel about the glorious Son of God becoming a citizen of earth. He has already lived here among us like other men, and He is a citizen of earth forevermore.

Christ's Humanity Is Eternal

Christ did not, in a transitory way, merely touch the human family, but He became forever identified with the race of Adam; He can never get away from His humanity. All that concerns our race concerns Him. He is a Man today, and He will be a Man forever; and, wherever mankind is to be, the Son of Man will be, also. Therefore, Christ's relationship to this old earth is a permanent one, and His kingdom is to be consummated here, where it first began.

There Are Still Prophecies to Be Fulfilled

Let us note that the promises and prophecies of the Old Testament have not been entirely satisfied and fulfilled. There is a double thread running through the warp and woof of ancient prophecy. There is the crimson line of the cross, but there is also the golden thread of the coming glory. The Jews saw only the prophecies of the glory; therefore, when Jesus appeared among them, they were not prepared to recognize the lowly Nazarene, that rejected Man, as the fulfillment of the splendid ideal. They had good cause for it, to a certain extent, at least. The only trouble with them was that they were out of date. They had mixed the chronology. He was the King, but He was not yet enthroned. It was first the cross and then the crown; first the Lamb of Calvary and then the Lion of the Tribe of Judah. Unless He comes again, part of the prophetic Scriptures will be unrealized. It was necessary that He should fulfill the vision of the cross, and it is just as necessary that He should fulfill the vision of the King.

There Is Christ's Own Testimony

When He was on earth, the Lord Jesus Himself always left the impression that He was coming back again—actually, visibly, personally—to His people. He also repeatedly told His disciples that when the Son of Man came, He would sit on the throne of His glory, and they would sit on thrones and receive rewards for their earthly sacrifice and sufferings. (See Matthew 19:28; 25:31–40.)

One particular event in the very middle of His career—the transfiguration on the mount—was an object lesson, a demonstration of this very thing, foreshadowing the fact that He who seemed so obscure was really to be unveiled someday in the great apocalypse of the second advent and appear in glory. The risen dead were represented by Moses, and the transfigured living by Elijah. (See Matthew 17:1–8; Mark 9:1–9.) In Matthew 24, we have a detailed prophecy of the Lord's return. We also have various parables: of the talents, the pounds, the marriage of the king's son, the ten virgins, and the sheep and the goats. These have no meaning unless the Lord is coming back again. All His teachings crystallized around two focal points—His cross and His second advent.

There Is Christ's Last Message

In the next place, Christ's very last message was on this specific subject. As He hovered in midair between earth and heaven, His parting word was sent back by two messengers (perhaps two glorified men) who stood by His followers and said, *"Why stand ye gazing up into heaven? This same Jesus…shall so come* [again] *in like manner as ye have seen him go into heaven"* (Acts 1:11). Put these three *s*'s together—*same, so, seen*—and you have a trinity of infallible proof. "*This same Jesus...shall so come...as ye have seen him go....*" He is the same, and He will be the same then—and we will see Him, and we will know He is the same. That is Christ's farewell message, and we know that He means what He says.

There Is the Testimony of the Apostles

The apostolic testimony was always the same. At the very beginning of the book of Acts, Peter said, "*Jesus Christ...whom the heaven must receive until the times of restitution of all things*" (Acts 3:20–21). Therefore, when that is accomplished, the heavens will not hold Him anymore.

Paul proclaimed Christ as the One who would be the Judge of the living and the dead. (See Romans 14:9.) In Romans, Paul gave three chapters (see Romans 9–11) to the dispensational questions leading up to the day when the Deliverer would come to Zion and "*turn away ungodliness from Jacob*" (Romans 11:26; see also Isaiah 59:20). The epistle of 1 Corinthians reaches its climax in the magnificent fifteenth chapter with the realities of that glorious appearing. (See 1 Corinthians 15:51–57.) Second Corinthians tells us how "*we must all appear before the judgment seat of Christ*" (2 Corinthians 5:10). Colossians tells us that "*when Christ...shall appear, then shall* [we] *also appear with him in glory*" (Colossians 3:4). First Thessalonians crystallizes around the doctrine of the Lord's coming. Every chapter and every important paragraph finds its keynote in this blessed hope. In 2 Timothy, Paul declared that it was his own personal hope that he would receive "*a crown of righteousness,*" which the Lord was keeping not only for him "*but unto all them also that love his appearing*" (2 Timothy 4:8). James bid us to be patient unto the coming of the Lord. (See James 5:8.) Peter told us it was the very meaning of the transfiguration when they "*were with him in the holy mount*" (2 Peter 1:18). John, in his epistles, and in the book of Revelation, repeated the message of

Christ's glorious second advent and the importance of our constant preparation for it.

There Is the Testimony of the Book of Revelation

But the supreme and crowning evidence of the Lord's premillennial coming is the glorious book of Revelation. Two generations after Christ had ascended, after thousands of saints had been gathered home, after hundreds of churches had been established on earth, after the spiritual facts and experiences of Christianity had been illustrated to the fullest extent, the Lord Himself came down as the last Messenger of inspired truth, and, to John on Patmos, He gave a glorious message, of which the keynote and finale is this: "I am coming again." The first announcement in Revelation is *"Behold, he cometh with clouds"* (Revelation 1:7), and the last farewell is *"Behold, I come quickly"* (Revelation 22:12; see also 22:20).

Will we answer, *"Even so, come* [quickly], *Lord Jesus"* (Revelation 22:20)?

CHAPTER TWO

THE CHRISTIAN AGE

*"He that hath an ear, let him hear what the Spirit saith
unto the churches."*
—Revelation 3:22

What is the prophetic preview of the present age, from the resurrection of Christ down to His second advent? This inquiry will throw much light upon many of the points that we have already touched on and make clearer, we trust, the utter unscripturalness of the postmillennial theory, or the prospect of a millennium without Christ.

The Church

The church belongs to the Christian age. It must be distinguished from Israel, God's Old Testament people. The church is the body of Christ, of which He is the Head, and the building of which He is the Cornerstone. Therefore, the church could not exist before Christ's finished work and resurrection. He said,

"Upon this rock [Himself] *I will build my church"* (Matthew 16:18). The church is *"built upon the foundation of the apostles and prophets, Jesus Christ himself being the chief corner stone"* (Ephesians 2:20). The real church, or body of Christ, is an invisible society, consisting of all who are born again and united to the Lord Jesus by the Holy Spirit, and who thus become partakers of His redemption and His life.

The visible church is the organized body of "those who profess and call themselves Christians." It is recognized in the New Testament as a divine organization, and yet, like every organization of imperfect human beings, it is also subject to imperfection and does not always correspond with the real spiritual body, which is truly united to Christ. The church, therefore, has its heresies, apostasies, and unfaithful members, as well as its true followers of the Lord Jesus. With various forms of government and standards of doctrine, it has existed throughout the Christian centuries and will exist until the Lord comes. It is the representative of the Lord on earth and His witness to the world, and, notwithstanding its imperfection, it enjoys the presence of the Master and the gifts and graces of the Pentecostal Spirit. And, through it, the Lord is gathering, one by one, the members of His body from every land in every generation.

The Church's Calling

The witnessing of the gospel to all nations is the business of the church in the present age:

> *Ye shall receive power after that the Holy Ghost is come upon you: and ye shall be witnesses unto me both in Jerusalem, and in all Judaea, and in Samaria, and unto the uttermost part of the earth.* (Acts 1:8)

*...and that repentance and remission of sins should be preached
in his name among all nations, beginning at Jerusalem. And
ye are witnesses of these things.*   (Luke 24:47–48)

*This gospel of the kingdom shall be preached in all the world
for a witness unto all nations; and then shall the end come.*
                                        (Matthew 24:14)

*God at the first did visit the Gentiles, to take out of them a
people for his name.*   (Acts 15:14)

These passages give a very explicit view of the special work of
the Holy Spirit and the church of Christ during the present age.
We are to be witnesses of Christ among all nations, first to the Jew
and then to the Gentile. (See Romans 1:16.) We are to preach the
gospel among all nations, not with the expectation that all will
be converted, but as a witness and an opportunity for salvation
for every sinful person. Through us, God is *visiting* the Gentiles,
not to continue their day of opportunity without limit, but for a
special time and purpose, that is, *"to take out of them a people for his
name."* He is sampling the families of humanity. He is gathering *"a
kind of firstfruits of his creatures"* (James 1:18) from every tribe and
tongue. In a word, He is constituting the bride of the Lamb of all
the races and kindreds and tongues of earth. And when the glorious day of His *parousia* comes, there will be *"a great multitude...of
all nations, and kindreds, and people, and tongues...before the throne,
and before the Lamb..."* (Revelation 7:9).

The Church's Failure

The Christian Age is not represented in the prophetic glimpses
given by Christ and His apostles as an age of ideal moral or spiritual perfection. On the contrary, there are early intimations of

error, declension, and apostasy. We find these things beginning even in the apostolic age; and, looking down to later times, the Lord Jesus told us,

> *Then shall many be offended, and shall betray one another, and shall hate one another. And many false prophets shall arise, and shall deceive many. And because iniquity shall abound, the love of many shall wax cold.*
>
> (Matthew 24:10–12)

Even the ministers of Christ will be like the evil servant who "*shall say in his heart, My lord delayeth his coming; and shall begin to smite his fellowservants, and to eat and drink with the drunken*" (Matthew 24:48–49). As it was in the days of Noah (and also of Lot), so shall it be in that day: "*They were eating and drinking, marrying and giving in marriage*" (Matthew 24:38; see also Luke 17:26–29), and wholly absorbed in the world's pleasures and cares.

In his letters to Timothy, the apostle Paul foretold the coming apostasy more explicitly:

> *This know also, that in the last days perilous times shall come. For men shall be lovers of their own selves, covetous, boasters, proud, blasphemers, disobedient to parents, unthankful, unholy, without natural affection, trucebreakers, false accusers, incontinent, fierce, despisers of those that are good, traitors, heady, highminded, lovers of pleasures more than lovers of God; having a form of godliness, but denying the power thereof.* (2 Timothy 3:1–5)

And again, still more emphatically, he told us,

> *The Spirit speaketh expressly, that in the latter times some shall depart from the faith, giving heed to seducing spirits, and doctrines of devils; speaking lies in hypocrisy; having their conscience seared with a hot iron; forbidding to marry, and commanding to abstain from meats, which God hath created*

*to be received with thanksgiving of them which believe and
know the truth.*   (1 Timothy 4:1–3)

Peter also, in his second epistle, forewarned us of the same
conditions:

*But there were false prophets also among the people [of Israel],
even as there shall be false teachers among you, who privily
shall bring in damnable heresies, even denying the Lord that
bought them, and bring upon themselves swift destruction.
And many shall follow their pernicious ways; by reason of
whom the way of truth shall be evil spoken of. And through
covetousness shall they with feigned words make merchandise
of you: whose judgment now of a long time lingereth not, and
their damnation slumbereth not.*   (2 Peter 2:1–3)

*Knowing this first, that there shall come in the last days scoff-
ers, walking after their own lusts, and saying, Where is the
promise of his coming? for since the fathers fell asleep, all things
continue as they were from the beginning of the creation.*
                                                    (2 Peter 3:3–4)

Jude also forecasted the same:

*But, beloved, remember ye the words which were spoken
before of the apostles of our Lord Jesus Christ; how that they
told you there should be mockers in the last time, who should
walk after their own ungodly lusts. These be they who separate
themselves, sensual, having not the Spirit.*   (Jude 17–19)

Already the fulfillment of these ominous forewarnings is
manifest on every hand. The church of the apostles became the
apostasy of Rome, and the church of the Reformation appears in
even greater danger of developing into the Laodicea of Revelation
(see Revelation 3:14–19), if not the Babylon of God's last and most
terrible judgment (see, for example, Revelation 14:8).

Parables of the Kingdom

Yet, the Lord Jesus has not left us mere fragments of prophetic foreshadowing; He has given us a very distinct unfolding of the progress of Christianity from the ascension to the second advent in the seven parables of the kingdom recorded in the thirteenth chapter of Matthew.

The disciples were looking for prosperity and popularity. They were delighted with the success of their Master—with His victory over disease, Satan, death, and sin. What power could resist Him? They already saw themselves sitting with Him on the thrones of David's restored kingdom. The Lord knew better. He saw the dark scenes that were just before them, and the centuries of suffering and seeming failure for the cause that He was establishing at such an awful cost. It was necessary that they should understand it, should be disillusioned, and should be sent forth as ministers of the New Testament with their eyes fully opened. It is a very dreadful thing today for a minister of the gospel to go forth expecting a brilliant future, expecting the acclamations of the crowd, expecting the people to applaud him because he is true to Jesus Christ.

It is necessary that the worker should understand that the kingdom of heaven always means the cross, the judgment hall, and the minority with the Lord Jesus Christ, our rejected Master. This was what He taught them in this series of parables. The parable of the sower represents the planting of Christianity. Three parts of the seed are lost, but one-fourth is productive, and the increase is thirtyfold, sixtyfold, and one hundredfold. (See Matthew 13:3–23.) They had to learn that most of their words would seem to fail, and there would be no response from the multitudes of hearts. From others, the fruit would be transient and soon forgotten. From still others, it would be lost in the temptations of the world. Only part of it would come to perfection. That is the first lesson the worker has to learn.

The parable of the tares represents the planting of error in the church—the heresies, corruptions, and interminglings of evil men in the early church, as well as in later times. (See Matthew 13:24–30.) Even the little that grew got mixed with Satan's seed. The disciples thought they could pull up the tares, but Jesus said that in pulling up the tares, they would pull up the wheat, also. The people who are in the business of judging are not in the Lord's employ. *"Let both grow together until the harvest"* (Matthew 13:30). Our dreams of a perfect church are doomed to be disappointed. The devil worked while the church was asleep—a work, alas, that we can ill eradicate by our discipline or denunciation; we must wait for much of it to be burned out at the great harvest time. Henceforth, the visible church is a mixture of truth and error, good and evil.

Next, in the parable of the mustard seed, we see the rapid growth of this mingled system covering the earth with its extensive shade and lodging the birds of heaven. (See Matthew 13:31–32.) Is not this most promising? Let us not be too sure. From the first parable, the birds of the air who lodge in the branches already have a bad reputation as the destructive and mischievous intruders who picked up the good seed; and here they would seem to be the same ill brood of evil emissaries who find shelter in the great, proud, worldly, and unhallowed church of the age of Constantine and today.

This is made much plainer when we come to the fourth parable, that of the leaven—which is God's uniform symbol of corruption. (See Matthew 13:33.) And when the woman is added to the picture, it becomes a significant and unmistakable emblem of the great apostasy that sprang up in the sixth and seventh centuries and speedily permeated the whole church with the leaven of the Papacy and all its kindred corruptions.

But was there no residue of good left of all the apostolic sowing? Yes, the parable of the hidden treasure (see

Matthew 13:44) and the parable of the pearl (see Matthew 13:45–46) represent the two sides of the elements of good, in contrast with the two symbols of evil. The treasure represents the pure and scriptural elements surviving in the church in the individuals—the many—while the pearl represents the church in its unity, as the one small yet pure and heavenly jewel of the Lord amid the encompassing corruption. Both find their historical fulfillment in the faithful few who have ever existed in even the darkest ages of medieval corruption: the Albigenses and Paulicians, the Hussites and Moravians, the Waldenses and Vaudois, the Wycliffites and Huguenots, the Reformers and Covenanters, and the pure and true ones who have before and since dared to be faithful to God and His holy Word. There has ever been a little flock, of which He says, *"They shall be mine... in that day when I make up my jewels"* (Malachi 3:17). There are some who identify the treasure with Israel and the pearl with the church, the bride of the Lamb. But this does not affect the dispensational bearing of the parables.

So far, have we seen the two sowings, the growth of the evil, and the hidden remnant of the good; and perhaps we ask, "Are they always to be thus mixed together?"

No, the parable of the draw net reveals to us the final separation. (See Matthew 13:47–50.) Angel hands will make it with impartial and unerring exactness, and these will be consigned to their eternal states and places: *"the righteous* [to] *shine forth as the sun in the kingdom of their Father"* (Matthew 13:43), and the wicked to *"the furnace of fire"* (Matthew 13:50).

The Seven Churches

Once more, in the seven epistles to the churches of Asia (see Revelation 1:10–3:22), our Lord's last word to the present age, we have what appears to the most thoughtful expositors a historical panorama of the successive stages of visible Christianity from the vision of Patmos to the end of time.

The seven churches correspond to the seven parables of the thirteenth chapter of Matthew. They teach the same lessons and unfold the same panorama, and we may well come to the solemn conclusion that the Master did after He had delivered them—*"He that hath an ear, let him hear what the Spirit saith unto the churches"* (Revelation 3:22)—for that is the last message of the Holy Spirit to the modern church. It was not the ancient church, not the apostolic church; it was the church that was on earth two generations after the death of Jesus. Thousands had gone to heaven. Thousands of churches had been organized. And now, at last, the Lord had come down to earth again for a second visitation in person; and, on the Isle of Patmos, He gave John a last revelation, a last outlook of the churches of the present age.

The wisest expositors have almost uniformly united in recognizing in these seven epistles a panorama stretching down from the days of John to the last time, each of these churches representing a different age, and yet each of them continuing in spirit to the end and adding a new coloring to the whole picture. They seem to meet like a great stream flowing down through church history. It begins in the church at Ephesus. Then we see another tributary running into it, the church of Smyrna. Then come Pergamos and Thyatira. Still later, Sardis pours its dark waters. Then follows the bright crystal river of Philadelphia; and, at last, it ends in a great sluggish swamp, Laodicea, which lies hard by the cities of the plain, Sodom and Gomorrah, and the gates of hell.

The church in Ephesus—orthodox, active, conservative, and growing cold—represents the second generation of the early Christians, already so far losing their first love that Paul and John alike spoke of this same Ephesian church as turning away from them. (See Revelation 2:1–7.)

The church in Smyrna is a suffering church, going through its ten days of tribulation, and purchasing, by blood and shame, the martyr's crown. (See Revelation 2:8–11.) This corresponds to the age of persecution that came in the second and third centuries to recall the cold and formal Ephesus to her first love, during which a series of ten distinct persecutions swept the whole line with fire and blood, and carried countless martyrs into heaven.

The church in Pergamos is a different type. It dwells at Satan's seat, the dominion of the world. It is assailed by Balaam's wiles, the allurements of the world. (See Revelation 2:12–17.) It was the church of Constantine and the converted empire—the church suddenly exalted to imperial favor, wealth, and power, and corrupted by the world from its faithfulness and purity until the smile of an emperor, the seat of honor at a banquet, the grand cathedral, and the proud bishopric or patriarchate took the place of ancient simplicity and fidelity, and prepared the way for the next and deeper plunge.

Then comes Thyatira, *"that woman Jezebel," "the depths of Satan"* (Revelation 2:20, 24), a true and vivid picture of the rise of Romanism and all its deep and devilish wiles and widespread domination over the church of God from the sixth to the sixteenth century. (See Revelation 2:18–29.)

Sardis represents a yet darker eclipse: *"Thou hast a name that thou livest, and art dead."* (See Revelation 3:1–6.) It was the Dark Ages, the putrid corpse of medieval Romanism.

And yet, in both these churches, there are a few exceptions— there is a holy seed. There are those in Thyatira who *"have not this doctrine, and which have not known the depths of Satan"* (Revelation 2:24); and there are *"a few names even in Sardis which have not defiled their garments"* (Revelation 3:4). These were the refugees of medieval times, the martyrs of Romanism, the witnesses for God before the Reformation, who suffered and died for the testimony of Jesus, to the number of countless millions.

Like a burst of sunrise comes the church in Philadelphia. It has *"a little strength"* (Revelation 3:8), but it is true. Especially does it honor God's Word and hold up Christ's name. Can we mistake it? It is the church of the Reformation, and its honored names will forever be as pillars in the temple of God and share the glories of the New Jerusalem. (See Revelation 3:7–13.)

But there is one chapter more (would that we did not have to write it). It is Laodicea, the church of wealth and pride, but so languid and lukewarm that the impatient Master is about to reject it as a nauseous offense. It is our modern Protestantism, boasting of its numbers, its works, its resources, while 149 out of every 150 of the human race are yet unsaved; while heathenism is increasing at the rate of two million a year; while one-sixtieth of one percent of our wealth is given for the gospel (and one-third is spent on whiskey and tobacco alone); while luxury, avarice, and pleasure are sapping the springs of piety and morality, and our culture is leading thousands into skepticism. The Master, in anger and concern, alternately pleads and warns, begs her to open the door and let Him in, threatens with rebukes and chastenings, and, with His hand on the very latch of time, is about to enter once more His temple and His world and make His last awful inquisition. (See Revelation 3:14–22.) And yet, He pauses, and, pointing to the millennial throne on which He is just about to sit down, He offers this glorious reward: *"To him that overcometh will I grant to sit with me in my throne, even as I also overcame, and am set down with My Father in His throne"* (Revelation 3:21).

Such is the picture of the church through the Christian Age. Have we understood all these things? Have we seen any family photographs? Are we ready for the inspection of Him who walks amid the seven golden lamps (see, for example, Revelation 4:5) and looks with eyes that are *"as a flame of fire"* (see, for example, Revelation 1:14)? Are we in Ephesus, Laodicea, or Pergamos—or, worse, in Thyatira or Sardis? Or, are we in suffering Smyrna or humble, faithful Philadelphia? Thank God, the seven churches are not merely for brief and transient periods, but the spirit of each continues to the end. So there is a holy Philadelphia even amid an insipid Laodicea. May He find us with the little flock to whom it is the Father's good pleasure to give the kingdom! (See Luke 12:32.)

CHAPTER THREE

THE WORLD POWERS

*"When the Most High divided to the nations their
inheritance, when he separated the sons of Adam,
he set the bounds of the people according to the number
of the children of Israel."*
—Deuteronomy 32:8

*"These great beasts, which are four, are four kings,
which shall arise out of the earth. But the saints of the most
High shall take the kingdom, and possess the kingdom
for ever, even for ever and ever....And the kingdom and
dominion, and the greatness of the kingdom under the whole
heaven, shall be given to the people of the saints of the most
High, whose kingdom is an everlasting kingdom, and all
dominions shall serve and obey him."*
—Daniel 7:17–18, 27

The plan of God embraces the political conditions of human
history. *"When the Most High divided to the nations their inheritance,*

when He separated the sons of Adam, he set the bounds of the people according to the number of the children of Israel" (Deuteronomy 32:8). The prophetic Scriptures contain a clear, distinct picture of national conditions throughout the ages and until the ushering in of the everlasting kingdom of our Lord and Savior Jesus Christ.

Soon after the deluge, human ambition made its first attempt to concentrate the race around one great metropolis of power and pride. The scene of this first attempt at imperial despotism afterward became the seat of the world's first universal empire, namely, Babylon. But the tower of Babel was stricken by divine judgment, and the nations scattered. (See Genesis 11:1–9.) It was fifteen centuries before any one of them succeeded in attaining universal empire. The prophetic Scriptures really begin, as far as the nations are concerned, with the rise of this first great world power—Babylon.

There are a number of important points that we should clearly understand in order to intelligently follow these prophetic Scriptures.

Prophetic Times

The first is the distinction between the times of the Gentiles and the times of the chosen people. In his solemn words of warning in the twenty-sixth chapter of Leviticus, Moses told the people that if they disobeyed the Lord and walked contrary to Him, He would punish them *"seven times"* for their disobedience. (See Leviticus 26:28.) This expression is repeated several times, until it is impossible to resist the conviction that it means much more than seven judgments but must embrace a particular period of trial and punishment whose duration is purposely expressed by this striking and significant phrase.

If this were the only place where the expression *seven times* was used, the above conclusion would not be so unavoidable, but we find the word *time* or *times* to be a standard measure of prophetic time; and, in other prophecies, we read again and again of "*a time*," "*times*," "*half a time*," and even "*seven times*." (See, for example, Daniel 4:16; 11:24; 12:7; Revelation 12:14.) Therefore, a large and important class of prophetic interpreters has come to the conclusion that a "time" is a fixed period and really means a year of 360 days, according to the solar calendar; "times" means two years of 360 days; and "seven times" means seven years of 360 days, or 2,520 days altogether. The same interpreters have concluded, on many satisfactory grounds, that, in this estimate of prophetic time, a day is counted for a year, so that 2,520 days means the same number of years. This is known as the Year-Day Theory of prophetic interpretation.

The fundamental argument for it is that in Daniel's prophecy, in the ninth chapter of his book, concerning the seventy weeks that should elapse until the arrival of Messiah (see Daniel 9:24), we have 490 days, and if these days are to be interpreted as literal days, the whole prophecy becomes impossible and absurd. But, if they are year-days, and the time covers 490 years, this corresponds exactly to the period that elapsed from Daniel's point of beginning to the coming of Christ. The evidence of this is so positive and unanswerable that, without the strongest reason to the contrary, it creates a precedent by which all other such prophetic measurements should be determined, unless there is, in any particular case, unquestionable proof that literal days are meant.

The Times of Israel

Without entering further into this argument, we will assume that the seven times of judgment that Moses was foreshadowing for Israel embraced a period of 2,520 years. We would naturally look for the beginning of that period in connection with the fall of the Jewish monarchy and the destruction of Jerusalem in the time of

Nebuchadnezzar, when Israel's independence as a nation virtually ceased, and the chosen people went down for ages under the dominion of the Gentile nations. From that day, the Jew has been down, and the Gentile has been in the ascendency, and Jerusalem has been *"trodden down"* (Luke 21:24) by the Gentiles until this day.

The Times of the Gentiles

The Lord Jesus described this period of Israel's being down-trodden as *"the times of the Gentiles"* (Luke 21:24). The apostle Paul used the same expression in the same connection, saying, *"I would not, brethren, that ye should be ignorant of this mystery, lest ye should be wise in your own conceits; that blindness in part is happened to Israel, until the fulness [times] of the Gentiles be come in"* (Romans 11:25). He implied what the Lord Jesus had also expressed in the passage quoted above—that when the times of the Gentiles will have been fulfilled, then Israel's times will be resumed. Therefore, he added, *"And so all Israel shall be saved: as it is written, There shall come out of [Zion] the Deliverer, and shall turn away ungodliness from Jacob"* (Romans 11:26).

But there is another passage that has special reference to the times of the Gentiles and that gives their duration. And, strangely enough, it is the same duration as the times of judgment pronounced against Israel. In other words, Israel is to have seven times of judgment, and, corresponding with these, the Gentile nations are to have seven times of dominion. When Israel is under the divine judgment, the star of the Gentiles is in the ascendant; when the times of the Gentiles end, then Israel's calling returns once more.

Nebuchadnezzar's Vision

This prophetic picture is given in the fourth chapter of Daniel in another vision of Nebuchadnezzar's, in which he saw the period of Gentile dominion represented under the figure of a tree over which seven times or periods were to pass. This was interpreted by Daniel to mean primarily a season of madness in Nebuchadnezzar's own life, which was to continue for seven times, or periods, during which he was to be degraded like the beasts of the field, at the end of which he was to be restored to his reason and take his place again—not as a proud and vainglorious king, but as a humble worshipper of the great God, recognizing His dominion over all kings and kingdoms. Inasmuch, however, as Nebuchadnezzar was himself but a type of his kingdom and the head of the kingdoms that were to follow, the ultimate fulfillment of this vision must be found in the whole history of the Gentile kingdoms. The bestial madness of Nebuchadnezzar represents just what Daniel's vision of the four wild beasts represented—the cruel, selfish, brutal, and earthly governments of the Gentile world, ruling over earth with a sort of madness, not as beneficent sovereigns but as ferocious wild beasts. They are destined in the purpose of God to continue their terrible control and their earthly character during seven great "times," or prophetic ages—2,520 years, or seven times of 360 years each; and, at the close of that great period, they will be restored from their gross and earthly madness by the coming of Christ and will recognize Him as "KING OF KINGS, AND LORD OF LORDS" (Revelation 19:16).

We now come to the prophetic picture of the times of the Gentiles in detail. This is given by the prophet Daniel in three remarkable visions in the second, seventh, and eighth chapters. So remarkable are the details that it reads more like history than prophecy, and its fulfillment is one of the strongest evidences of the inspiration of the Bible, so that even secular writers have acknowledged the wonderful correspondence between the visions of Daniel and the facts of history.

The Image of Gentile Power

In the second chapter of Daniel's writings, we find the first complete chart of the world's political future until the close of the present dispensation. It was given first to Nebuchadnezzar in a forgotten dream of his troubled sleep. Afterward, it was revealed to Daniel and interpreted by him in the presence of the king. Under the figure of a great image in the form of a man—with head of gold, arms and breast of silver, loins of brass, legs of iron, and feet and toes of iron and clay—he beheld the symbols of the four great empires that, in succession, were to rule the world until the end, as well as the broken kingdoms to the number of ten that were to rise out of the last of the four empires and close the drama of the Gentile nations. The head of gold was declared to represent the splendid empire of which Nebuchadnezzar was himself the living head. The arms and breast of silver foreshadowed the Medo-Persian Empire, which was to conquer and subdue Babylon. The loins of brass prefigured the strong empire of Alexander and his successors. The legs of iron were the fitting type of the Roman power, with its all-subduing might. And the feet and toes of iron and clay represented the smaller kingdoms that were to rise out of the ruins of the Roman Empire and close the history of earth's governments.

The audacity of a captive daring to tell a despot like Nebuchadnezzar in the meridian of his glory that his kingdom could ever fall is the strongest evidence of the divinity of the message. The picture is marvelously true to the facts of history. Babylon was actually the first head of universal monarchy, having conquered Nineveh in the year 667 BC, and holding the scepter of the world until her own fall before the Medo-Persians in 538 BC. This second empire, in turn, swayed a still larger circle of dominion until it was superseded by the Macedonian in 332 BC under Alexander. It, in turn, gradually fell before the Roman power, which had begun its career in the year 753 BC and absorbed all other nations until, at length, the last independent remnant of the Macedonian Empire fell before it a little before the Christian era. Rome, in turn, divided into the Western and Eastern empires, which successively fell before other invaders—the one in AD 476 and the other in AD 1453. And it was succeeded by a cluster of smaller kingdoms, which, at all times since the fall of Rome, and especially at the present time, could truthfully be enumerated as ten, and singularly correspond to the toes upon the feet of the image—Great Britain, France, Germany, Austria, Spain and Portugal, Scandinavia, the Netherlands, Turkey, Russia, and Italy. These ten kingdoms constitute what is left of the old Roman Empire.

Moreover, we observe that the materials composing the image in its several parts are singularly suggestive of these successive empires. Gold was the correct emblem of the magnificence of Babylon; silver of the luxurious elegance of Persia; brass of the tremendous vigor of Macedonia; iron of the colossal power of Rome; and clay of the brittle, fragile, heterogeneous, and changing character of the later kingdoms. Moreover, we see a constant tendency to degeneration from Babylon downward. This is especially marked in the matter of national unity. Babylon was a single power; Persia was a double power; Macedonia divided into four kingdoms; and Rome terminated in ten, as we will see from later prophetic visions. Even these ten seem to end at last in universal democracy.

The Stone

One more feature appears, and it is the most strongly marked of all in this first vision—namely, a stone cut out without hands that falls upon the image, smiting it upon the toes, crushing them to powder and scattering them like chaff before the winds, while the stone becomes a great and permanent kingdom, filling all the earth and superseding all other forms of human government. This stone is distinctly declared to represent the kingdom of Christ. Had it come in a different form, to blend with the materials of the image or to incorporate them into its substance, or had it even fallen upon the legs of iron, it might have been interpreted to mean the first coming of Christ, the gospel dispensation and the conversion of the world. But it comes in the very last stage of earth's nations, smiting the toes; and it comes not to coalesce but to destroy. It must, therefore, mean the second advent of the Son of God at the close of time. It is a revelation of judgment and destruction toward the enemies of the gospel—coming not to convert and purify but to supersede the governments of earth and to be a kingdom more enduring than all the kingdoms of the past.

The Wild Beast Powers of Daniel 7

But this was not the only vision that Daniel saw of earth's political future. A second series of symbolic visions of the same great empires was given to him at a later period of his writings. In the former vision, the powers of earth were represented from Nebuchadnezzar's standpoint, as objects of magnificence, and under the symbols of earth's most precious and valued metals. But in the later visions in the seventh chapter—which were Daniel's visions, not Nebuchadnezzar's—heaven beholds these forms of earthly power and pride under the repulsive images of terrible wild beasts. The first, representing the supremacy, majesty, and rapid conquests of Babylon, is a winged lion, which, indeed, we find among the ruins of Babylon as one of the national emblems. The second, a ferocious bear, with three ribs in its teeth, represents the savage cruelty of Persia. This was the nation that could produce a Haman, and decree the massacre of the whole Jewish population in a single hour, and cast even Daniel into the den of lions—the nation that devoured and destroyed three kingdoms as it rose to its preeminence. The third is a winged leopard with four heads, representing the swiftness of Alexander's conquests and the four kingdoms that succeeded him. The fourth is a monster of indescribable form and terror—with teeth of iron and heels that stamped in fury all other powers beneath its feet—representing the fourth great power, namely, Rome, which crushed the world beneath its feet, stamped out the independence of Judea and other nations, crucified the Son of God, captured and crushed Jerusalem, and murdered tens of millions of Christian martyrs in the first three centuries. Then, corresponding to the ten toes in the former vision, there are also ten horns, rising out of the fourth beast, which undoubtedly represent the same ten kingdoms that we have already defined and that succeeded after the fall of imperial Rome.

The Ram and He-Goat Powers of Daniel 8

In the eighth chapter of Daniel, we have a third vision of two of the powers that have already been described. The two empires thus portrayed are Persia and Macedonia. The first is represented by a ram, and the second by a he-goat, characterized by the notable horn between his eyes, representing Alexander the Great. At length, this horn was broken and was followed by the growth of four lesser horns, which represent the four kingdoms into which Alexander's empire divided. In the prophetic vision, the ram and the he-goat meet in terrific and decisive conflict. The former is speedily worsted and stamped out of existence, and the second succeeds to the sway of his universal empire. This, of course, describes the fall of Persia before the Grecian conqueror. But the emphatic feature of the vision is the importance attached to one of these four horns and to a little horn that grows out of it, which, in later days, becomes a proud, presumptuous, and oppressive power, especially in the eastern and southern portions of the world, as the little horn of the seventh chapter had been in the western and Roman world.

The Visions of John's Revelation

In the book of Revelation, we have a remarkable series of visions respecting the world powers in connection with the coming of Christ. These are found especially in chapters thirteen, seventeen, and eighteen. In Revelation 13, the beloved John beholds a vision strangely similar to Daniel's. It is the vision of the last of Daniel's beasts—with the addition (besides the ten horns) of seven dreadful heads, and the further addition of the dragon in the background—as the real master and moving spirit of the whole procession of earth's powers and governments. The beast that John beheld was the same that Daniel had prefigured. Its seven heads were the seven successive forms of Roman government, and its last head was the same apostasy that Daniel saw as a little horn and that succeeded to the power of imperial Rome after the fall of the western empire. John beheld the same ten kingdoms growing out of the Roman beast.

Last-Day Democracies

There are some peculiar features, however, with regard to this vision and John's subsequent visions, that deserve to be noted. One of these is that, in his first view of the horns, there are crowns upon all their heads. In his later visions, they are seen without their crowns. This, coupled with other expressions, such as *"many waters"* (Revelation 17:1), seems to indicate that, in the last days, the governments of earth will be democratic (and probably even anarchical and lawless) and that the world is rapidly rushing to an age of license, whose first symptoms are already only too apparent in the popular and socialistic movements of Europe and America alike.

Another feature in the visions of Revelation is the relationship of the nations to the great apostasy of Rome. They are represented in the first period of her career as sustaining this ecclesiastical system represented by the woman on the scarlet-colored beast and being united with her in unholy alliance. But later, we see them hating her, ravaging her, and resenting fiercely her long and arrogant dominance over them. This also has been strangely true during the past ten centuries and is being literally fulfilled in Europe today in such Roman Catholic countries as Italy, France, and Portugal.

One more important feature of the national history of the future is very distinctly portrayed in Revelation—namely, the relationship of the nation to Christ and His cause and the last great struggle between good and evil toward the close of the present age. The spirit of evil that rules in the powers of earth is to send forth a deluge of unhallowed influences, represented by *"three unclean spirits like frogs"* (Revelation 16:13), which will go forth to possess the minds and hearts of the kings and peoples of earth with bitter and wicked hatred toward God and to gather them together for the last great conflict against Christ and His cause. This is described as the war of Armageddon. (See Revelation 16:13–16.) There, the proud and godless hosts of earth will make their final stand against Christ and His people. It will be much more than a moral and spiritual struggle; it will be a literal battle against the Jewish nation and the Lamb of God. The result cannot be doubtful. The glorious appearing of the Son of God will end the conflict, and before His tribunal all nations will be gathered for the judgment that is to determine their place of destiny during the Millennial Age.

CHAPTER FOUR

GOD'S PLAN FOR ISRAEL

*"When the Most High divided to the nations their
inheritance, when he separated the sons of Adam,
he set the bounds of the people according to the number of the
children of Israel. For the LORD's portion is his people;
Jacob is the lot of his inheritance."*
—Deuteronomy 32:8–9

*"The people shall dwell alone, and shall not be reckoned
among the nations."*
—Numbers 23:9

The existence and history of the Jewish nation are a stupendous monument to the truth of the Bible. The seed of Abraham is God's miracle in history. The Jewish people dwell among the nations— *"alone…among* [them]" but not of them. Like oil in water, they are distinct from, and above the surface of, the many peoples where they have been scattered.

The Calling and Mission of Israel

We find a sketch of God's plan for Israel in the ninth, tenth, and eleventh chapters of Romans. Paul paused in his great treatise to give us three chapters of dispensational truth in which the Jews loom large in God's eternal plan. Speaking of the Israelites, he said, "*To whom pertaineth the adoption* [sonship], *and the glory...*" (Romans 9:4). They are the only nation that was ever called the sons of God. Socialism talks about the fatherhood of God and the brotherhood of man. Christ tells us that we are children of the devil until we are born from above. (See John 8:44–47.)

As a nation, the Jews were the sons of God. Israel was the first-born to whom pertained the sonship and the glory, which God gave to them under David and Solomon, and which He is going to give to them again. All the promises of God came through them. All our ethical standards come to us from them.

> *To whom pertaineth the adoption, and the glory, and the covenants, and the giving of the law, and the service of God, and the promises; whose are the fathers, and of whom as concerning the flesh Christ came, who is over all, God blessed for ever. Amen.* (Romans 9:4–5)

This, then, was the calling of the Jews. This was the high place God intended for them. First, they were to be the depositories of divine truth, to receive and distribute to the world the light of heaven. In the next place, Israel was to be a witness for God among the nations and an object lesson showing God's relations with humanity; for through His dealing with them, God has unfolded His principles of government over all nations. They were separated from association with the ungodly world. They received the covenants. They gave us Jesus Christ, "*of whom as concerning the flesh Christ came.*" All this we owe to Israel, a debt we never can repay. If it had not been for the Jews, we would have no Bible, no Christ, and no covenants of promise.

The nation was called in the loins of Abraham and was given to him in covenant as a literal posterity as numerous as the sand upon the seashore (see Genesis 22:17; 32:12), accompanied by the promise of the land for *"an everlasting possession"* (Genesis 17:8; 48:4). Abraham has a spiritual seed too, *"as the stars of heaven"* (Genesis 26:4; see also Genesis 22:17). But God is not going to let the spiritual seed steal their brethren's earthly inheritance. As believers in Christ, we are the spiritual seed of Abraham, for Abraham is *"the father of all them that believe* (Romans 4:11). But, in receiving our spiritual privileges, let us not push out the Jews from their earthly inheritance. While ours is assured by the covenants of God, for them, the same covenants are *"without repentance"* (Romans 11:29) and cannot be abrogated.

God renewed His covenant with Jacob, Moses, Samuel, David, and Solomon; in Solomon the kingdom rose to its highest earthly glory. We read in David's last words, *"Although my house be not so with God; yet he hath made me an everlasting covenant, ordered in all things, and sure"* (2 Samuel 23:5). In Psalm 89, this covenant is renewed and confirmed forever:

> *If his children forsake my law, and walk not in my judgments; if they break my statutes and keep not my commandments; then will I visit their transgression with the rod, and their iniquity with stripes. Nevertheless, my lovingkindness will I not utterly take from him, nor suffer my faithfulness to fail. My covenant will I not break, nor alter the thing that is gone out of my lips. Once have I sworn by my holiness that I will not lie unto David. His seed shall endure for ever, and his throne as the sun before me.* (Psalm 89:30–36)

We are taught very clearly in the epistle to the Romans that God is not going to change this covenant, and even Israel's ill conduct has not dissolved it. They are being punished, but God will be true to His oath. Thus, we read,

> *And so all Israel shall be saved: as it is written, There shall*
> *come out of [Zion] the Deliverer, and shall turn away ungod-*
> *liness from Jacob: for this is my covenant unto them, when I*
> *shall take away their sins....For the gifts and calling of God*
> *are without repentance.* (Romans 11:26–27, 29)

The Failure and Rejection of Israel

We find even Moses looking forward to this in his last warnings to the Israelites. For forty years, they had to wander in the
wilderness; and later, for four hundred years after Joshua, they
had to be disciplined and punished again. They had had a greater
blessing, and, therefore, they had a greater fall. Samuel was called
to restore them in the great reformation, which he brought about.
And David became their divinely appointed king and victorious
leader in acquiring the promised kingdom. He extended his scepter over a vast area, and the kingdom of Judah and Israel was not
only the most powerful on earth but was also worthy to be compared with any modern nation. Solomon succeeded to it, and, for
a time, he was worthy of his glorious throne; but Solomon's heart
became corrupted by luxury and the influence of ungodly associ-
ates, and God had to send the severest judgments upon His people.

After Solomon's death, the division of the people by the
rebellion of Jeroboam resulted in Solomon's son inheriting only
two tribes; the other ten became a separate monarchy under the
northern kings, with their capital at Samaria. These two kingdoms moved on side by side for several centuries, both sinking
deeper into idolatry, until, finally, the northern kingdom became
so utterly apostate that God had to send upon it a terrific judgment that literally wiped it from the face of the earth. He sent
the Assyrians to capture Samaria, and the land was given up to
foreign races. From that day, the world has been wondering what

has become of the ten tribes of Israel. Apparently, they have been utterly blotted from the pages of history.

For a few centuries longer, the southern kingdom lingered, with its story of sinning and repenting. A few kings tried to lift it back to the plane where David and Solomon had left it, but at last they all failed. Then came another blow—the Babylonian captivity. God sent Nebuchadnezzar against Jerusalem, and after a succession of calamities lasting nearly twenty years, the city was captured, the temple burned, and the people led away captive for seventy years.

In His infinite mercy and faithfulness, God gave them another chance. Under Joshua, Ezra, and Nehemiah, they were restored to their land. Under the Maccabees, they fought for their independence and flung off the yoke of their oppressor for a time. And when Jesus came, there still was the form of a kingdom, although the sovereign was a dependent of Rome. But the scepter had not wholly departed from Judah. (See Genesis 49:10.)

Then they rejected and crucified the Messiah. His tears and warnings were unavailing as He told them, *"Behold, your house is left unto you desolate"* (Matthew 23:38)—the enemy would encamp about them and capture their fair city, and *"Jerusalem [would] be trodden down"* (Luke 21:24) for centuries, and Israel scattered among the nations.

Israel's Punishment

Very soon, the judgment fell. He gave them a short probation during the first few years of the apostles' ministry. He even sent Paul to them for a final appeal, but they rejected him:

[Paul and Barnabas said,] *It was necessary that the word of God should first have been spoken to you: but seeing ye put it from you, and judge yourselves unworthy of everlasting life, lo, we turn to the Gentiles.*   (Acts 13:46)

Paul was pressed in the spirit, and testified to the Jews that Jesus was Christ. And when they opposed themselves, and blasphemed, he shook his raiment, and said unto them, Your blood be upon your own heads; I am clean: from henceforth I will go unto the Gentiles. (Acts 18:5–6)

Then, the Roman eagles began to gather around the doomed city of Jerusalem. It was besieged for two dreadful years, and finally it fell—after many preternatural signs, of which Josephus, their own historian, has told us. The city was sacked and burned and ploughed over so that the temple site might be obliterated. We can still see the inscription on the Arch of Titus, showing the Roman soldiers carrying the golden candlestick as a trophy of their triumph.

Forty years later, another Jewish rebellion arose to try to throw off the Roman yoke. Yet, they were not only subdued but also utterly crushed, and the Jews were forbidden to ever look toward Jerusalem, on penalty of death. Half a million Jews were butchered by the Roman emperors Trajan and Hadrian, and then the Jews' night of sorrow dragged its slow length through medieval centuries.

Medieval Cruelties

After Constantine's conversion and the establishment of Christianity through the empire, the Jews became the object of aversion and oppression. They were regarded as the murderers of Christ and treated as criminals and outlaws. Eventually, the Saracens joined the Christians in this common hatred of the poor Hebrews. In the eleventh century, they were banished from England. In the same century, the crusade of the Holy War began against the Jews, compelling them to be baptized or slain, and multitudes of Jews were murdered all over Germany. In the twelfth century, they were banished from France, with all their property confiscated. In England, under the reigns of Henry II and Richard I, they suffered every kind of extortion and barbarity; and, in the reign of Edward I, they were again banished. King John and many of his successors tortured them until they confessed and yielded up their treasures. In the year of the discovery of America, 800,000 Jews were driven from Spain amid every kind of privation and distress, not even knowing where to turn their weary feet. Multitudes slew their own children to save them from horrors that were worse than death. In 1543, 5,000 Jews, with all their effects and synagogues, were burned at Salonika. In Constantinople, the Jews' quarter was burned, with 3,000 houses destroyed and $60 million of their property plundered. And so the sad and sickening story goes on. We cannot better sum it up than in these words:

A Jewish calendar, with a chronological table, forming "a summary of Jewish history from the flood to the year 1860," lies before us. We run the eye questioningly over its pages, and what do we find as we review the incidents of this second section of Jewish history there recorded? An unconscious acknowledgment from Jewish pens that every threat of judgment denounced against Israel in case of continued rebellion and idolatry, by Moses and the prophets, has been fulfilled. An acknowledgment that ever since their fall before the power of Babylon, in the sixth century BC, they have been in subjection to Gentile rulers; and that since AD 135 they have been dispersed among all nations; that their history has consisted of one long chain of great and sore calamities, interrupted only with brief gleams of passing prosperity. They have been exposed to innumerable evils of every kind: to famines and plagues, captivities and banishments without number, to social distress and degradation, to outlawry and the hatred of their Gentile neighbours, to false accusations and frequent massacres, to exactions and imposts almost exceeding belief, to pillage and torture, to the most painful forms of social ostracism and injustice; in a word, that they have been so relentlessly crushed down by their Gentile masters, that existence itself would have been crushed out of them long since but for the strange indestructibility with which, in the providence of God, their race is endowed....[2]

Truly has it been said,

> The wild-dove hath her nest, the fox his cave,
> Mankind their country—Israel but the grave![3]

The Outcast Nation

It is only within about one hundred years that the Jew has been allowed any sort of citizenship in any nation under heaven. The light is beginning to dawn at last; but, oh, how little the Jewish people who called for Christ's crucifixion realized what they meant when they said, on that awful day, *"His blood be on us, and on our children"* (Matthew 27:25). Let Moses tell the prophetic story:

> *And the* LORD *shall scatter thee among all people, from the one end of the earth even unto the other; and there thou shalt serve other gods, which neither thou nor thy fathers have known, even wood and stone. And among these nations shalt thou find no ease, neither shall the sole of thy foot have rest: but the* LORD *shall give thee there a trembling heart, and failing of eyes, and sorrow of mind: and thy life shall hang in doubt before thee; and thou shalt fear day and night, and shalt have none assurance of thy life: in the morning thou shalt say, Would God it were even! and at even thou shalt say, Would God it were morning! for the fear of thine heart wherewith*

*thou shalt fear, and for the sight of thine eyes which thou shalt
see.*   (Deuteronomy 28:64–67)

That is all true of the Jews in Russia today. Five million of
them in that empire are confined in a little section called the Pale.
They dare not move out of their territory, except by special license;
and that is given only occasionally to rich men. They are liable to
assassination and outrage at any time. The past decade has given
us the horrors of Kishinev, and similar records of oppression and
wrong cover their history for nearly twenty centuries.

The only light in this sad picture is suggested by the story of
two rabbis who were watching the ruins of Jerusalem one day as
the foxes were running over the walls. The one wept and the other
smiled.

"Brother, why dost thou weep?" asked the smiling one.

"I weep because I see the foxes running over the walls of the
city of my fathers. Why dost thou smile?"

"I smile because this is what God said should come to pass,
and the word of promise is as true as the word of judgment, for He
has also said, 'Jerusalem shall yet be the joy of the whole earth.'"

A Remnant

God has said that though the Jews be scattered like seed
among all nations, yet not one grain will be lost. Again, He said
that during this present age, a remnant will be saved. While the
nation has rejected Christ, there are yet some who believe in Him.
*"Though the number of the children of Israel be as the sand of the sea,
a remnant shall be saved"* (Romans 9:27). *"Even so then at this present time also there is a remnant according to the election of grace"*
(Romans 11:5). A few have been accepting Christ all through the
centuries. We are told by Jewish mission workers that there are at
least 50,000 Jewish converts today in the churches of Europe. That

is very encouraging. Some of the most gifted Bible scholars, teachers, and defenders of the Christian faith are Hebrews. Some of the most earnest and eloquent ministers of the gospel of Jesus Christ are both of the Jewish race and of the Christian faith. Jewish mission work is not the principal work of the church, but it is one of its commissions: *"To the Jew first, and also to the Greek"* (Romans 1:16). We must not let this work monopolize us. If we do, we will be disappointed. We must remember that the spiritual Israel is *"a remnant."* This is not Israel's day, but God is saving some even today, and we ought to be doing all we can to give them the gospel.

Israel's Restoration

Then there is the promise of their restoration. This is to be in two stages: first, national; then, spiritual. These two stages are represented by Ezekiel in the vision of the dry bones. Here is the first stage:

> [The Lord] *caused me to pass by* [the bones] *round about: and, behold, there were very many in the open valley; and, lo, they were very dry. And he said unto me, Son of man, can these bones live?…Then he said unto me, Son of man, these bones are the whole house of Israel: behold, they say, Our bones are dried, and our hope is lost: we are cut off for our parts.* (Ezekiel 37:2–3, 11)

However, God has promised to revive the nation and to bring the people to the land of their fathers.

> *Thus saith the Lord GOD; Behold, O my people, I will open your graves, and cause you to come up out of your graves, and bring you into the land of Israel. And ye shall know that I am the LORD, when I have opened your graves, O my people, and brought you up out of your graves….* (Ezekiel 37:12–13)

But that is all physical—there is no breath in them. So, here is the second stage of Israel's restoration:

> *Again he said unto me, Prophesy upon these bones, and say unto them, O ye dry bones, hear the word of the LORD. Thus saith the Lord GOD unto these bones; Behold, I will cause breath to enter into you, and ye shall live.…Then said he unto me, Prophesy unto the wind, prophesy, son of man, and say to the wind, Thus saith the Lord GOD; Come from the four winds, O breath, and breathe upon these slain, that they may live. So I prophesied as he commanded me, and the breath came into them, and they lived, and stood up upon their feet, an exceeding great army.* (Ezekiel 37:4–5, 9–10)

Israel is to be restored not only to their land but also to their Messiah. "*And [I] shall put my spirit in you, and ye shall live, and I shall place you in your own land: then shall ye know that I the LORD have spoken it, and performed it, saith the LORD*" (Ezekiel 37:14).

Deliverance Begun

God has begun these two stages of His work in the restoration of Israel. During the past two centuries, every country in Europe except Russia and Turkey has adopted measures leading to the enfranchisement of the Jews. In 1844, the Turkish empire was compelled to sign a decree giving permission for Jews and Christians and all others to enjoy religious liberty, and, a little later, the right to own property in their land. This was just 2,300 years after the decree of Artaxerxes in 457 BC, the initial point of Daniel's prophecy; and thus it was a marked fulfillment of that prophecy.

In 1860, a Hebrew alliance was formed with some three thousand branches throughout the whole world for the purpose of uniting the Jews in demanding their civic and other social privileges.

Today, that is one of the most powerful influences for the protection of the Jews. They did not yet dream of returning to their own land.

Zionism

But, in 1897, a most extraordinary movement was launched—Zionism—and, ever since, that society has been growing in numbers and influence. In addressing the delegates of the congress where Zionism was formed, Max Nordau said, "It seemed as if we were witnessing a miracle." The most extraordinary thing about this great event was that it corresponded exactly with another of Daniel's prophecies. In Daniel 12:7, God had said that the scattering of the Jewish people would cease after 1,260 years. Then, they were to begin to unite and gather home. In the year AD 637, Omar, the victorious general of Muhammad, captured the city of Jerusalem.[4] From that time, the Muslims have been in dominion. As he entered the city, the old Bishop Sophronius, with tears and sobs, cried, "The abomination of desolation, spoken of by Daniel the prophet, is set up." And sure enough, it was. On the site of the temple of Solomon, a mosque was raised for Islamic worship. Ever since, Jerusalem has been trodden down by the Muslims, and the holy people scattered and crushed under their iron heel. From AD 637, 1,260 years (Daniel's *"time, times, and an half"*) brings us to the year 1897. And that was the year when the Zionist conference founded the great society whose watchword ever since has been this: The Jew must be restored, and Israel must again become a nation.

There is no need for comment on such a record. How long it will take God to finish the restoration of Israel, we cannot tell. But the political restoration has begun. The dry bones are coming together, although there is yet no breath. It is a political society without God.

The Coming Deliverer

The Jews are going back—going back in unbelief, going back in national pride; yet *"they shall look upon [Him] whom they have pierced; and they shall mourn for him"* (Zechariah 12:10; see also John 19:37). *"In that day there shall be a fountain opened to the house of David and to the inhabitants of Jerusalem for sin and uncleanness"* (Zechariah 13:1). *"And there shall come out of [Zion] the Deliverer, and shall turn away ungodliness from Jacob"* (Romans 11:26). The unbelieving Jews will behold Him when He comes to gather His church and bride; they will catch a passing glimpse of the glory of His train, and they will say, "This is our Messiah, and we have rejected Him. We have lost Him!" And they will mourn because of Him. In the tribulation that will follow, two-thirds will be destroyed, but one-third will survive and will come out on the other side in the millennial morning and be the beginning of a new Jewish nation that will last throughout the coming age of glory.

The Final Conflict and the Millennial Age

The last chapters of Zechariah and Daniel describe the awful conflict that is to come to the Jews in the last hour of their sorrow, *"the time of Jacob's trouble"* (Jeremiah 30:7). The Son of God will appear, standing with His feet on Mount Olivet (see Zechariah 14:4), to deliver them from their adversaries and to set up a throne of David again on the millennial earth. The following eloquent passage may help us to realize the picture of that future age:

Beyond the immediate prospects in relation to the Jews and Palestine rises the glowing and glorious picture of the future of that people and land, as portrayed in scripture, and illuminated by a study of the physical conditions, and ethnographical surroundings involved. Placed at the junction of three continents, and at the gateway of commerce between the West and the East; possessed of tropical valleys, and snow-clad mountains, the land of the palm and the cedar, of the olive and the vine, holds forth its hands of promise to the wandering, exiled Jews. Carmel and Sharon covered in spring with their roses, the fields of Bethlehem, and hills of Nazareth with their anemones, the plain of Esdraelon with its corn-fields, the Jordan valley with its luxuriant foliage, the wilds of Bashan with their pastures, all wait for the Jewish hands and homes which are yet to cultivate and occupy them. The long neglected Gulf of Akaba with its noble headlands projecting into the Red Sea shall yet become a highway of commerce to southern Palestine. Ezion-geber at the head of that gulf will be connected by railway with the Dead Sea, the Jordan valley, and the Lake of Gennesareth. The waters of Merom and sources of the Jordan shall be linked with the crowded streets of Damascus and the snow-clad steeps of Hermon. The slopes of Lebanon will be populated, and the city of Antioch revived. Beyrout, already connected with the ports of the Mediterranean and with Damascus, shall be the gate of a highroad through the Euphrates valley to the Persian Gulf, India, and the East. Africa traversed with railways shall lie at the feet of Palestine, and Europe with its wealth of civilization shall flourish at its side. The Jews restored from all countries, and speaking all languages, shall be fitted for the work of evangelizing the world. Their marvellous commercial, political, and literary gifts shall come into fullest play. No more shall they be a despised and outcast people. The natural brethren, the blood relations of the King of Glory, shall take a foremost place among the nations. The sigh of sorrow, the wail of grief shall be turned to the song of gladness, and the shout of praise. The voice of redeeming love and mercy shall swell from innumerable multitudes; Jerusalem shall vibrate with its music, Carmel prolong its cadence, and Lebanon echo back its strains. The song of angels shall awake again above the fields of Bethlehem; and heaven and earth unite their voices as never before in the anthem which shall celebrate the triumph of redeeming grace and mercy.[5]

CHAPTER FIVE

THE GREAT APOSTASY

In the vision of Daniel 7, the figure that most impressed the mind of the prophet and held his spellbound gaze, even after the other images had passed out of view, was not the winged lion, the devouring bear, the four-headed leopard, or even the strange and terrible monster with teeth of iron. Neither was it the ten horns that grew out of its mighty head; it was that other horn, the *"little horn"* (Daniel 7:8)…

> which came up, and before whom three [other horns] fell; even of that horn that had eyes, and a mouth that spake very great things, whose look was more stout than his fellows. Until the Ancient of days came, and judgment was given to the saints of the most High; and the time came that the saints possessed the kingdom….The same horn made war with the saints, and prevailed against them….He shall be diverse from the first, and he shall subdue three kings. And he shall speak great words against the most High, and shall wear out the saints of the

most High, and think to change times and laws: and they shall
be given into his hand until a time and times and the dividing
of time. But the judgment shall sit, and they shall take away
his dominion, to consume and to destroy it unto the end.

(Daniel 7:20–22, 24–26)

If we have been right in our interpretation of the fourth beast
and the horns as denoting Rome and the divided kingdoms that
grew out of it, then it is evident that this other horn, which is thus
prominently described, must be some power that arose simultane-
ously with the fall of Rome and the rise of these ten kingdoms.
It must be a power that is in some important sense diverse from
them and yet like them, a power that subverted three of the contemporary kingdoms, a power that became the persecutor of the
saints of God, a power that was to last for 1,260 years, and a power
that God was, at the end, to sit in judgment upon and gradually
consume and destroy.

Is there anything in history that corresponds to this description? Rather, is there any possibility of mistaking the identity of
the only figure that corresponds to this vivid prophetic-historical
picture? Is this not a living photograph of the origin and progress
of the papal power as it has filled up the last thirteen centuries and
made itself, as it was in Daniel's vision, the most marked and striking picture of medieval and modern history?

Let us notice in detail the points of identity as given in Daniel's
vision, and then in the visions of Paul and John.

Daniel's Picture

1. It was to be a horn out of the fourth beast. Now, the Papacy
sprang out of Rome. Its very roots are fastened in the seven hills.
Its very cornerstone is Peter's ministry and primacy in Rome. The
empire of the popes succeeded to the empire of the Caesars and

saved the city from obscurity and desolation. It could not arise in all its supremacy till Rome fell; and, when the western empire was shattered, the popes inherited its authority and power over the Roman states.

2. It was to be an actual horn, a real state, a political power. And so the Papacy has been for more than twelve centuries. It has had a twofold form as distinct as the offices of Moses and Aaron. It has been a temporal kingdom and an ecclesiastical body, priest-hood, and church. It is in the first of these aspects that Daniel views it, as a political power, an actual horn. It is only since 1870 that this form of its existence has passed away.

3. It was to be *"diverse"* (Daniel 7:24) from the other horns. It is not necessary to show how distinctively Rome has differed from all other states in its particular character and claims, professing to be a divine government and combining both the civil and sacer-dotal functions and assumptions. No other such government has ever existed or ever wielded such tremendous power.

4. It was to arise after the other horns. And so the temporal power of the Papacy slowly took shape after the fall of Rome and the division of the western empire. And, although it began about the sixth century, it was not fully consolidated until the time of Pepin III, in the eighth century.

5. It was to subdue three kings. And so the Papacy literally did absorb and supersede, successively, the following: first, Odoacer and the Heruli; second, the Ostrogoths; and, third, the Lombards.

6. It was to be a little horn. Accordingly, the Papal States were always territorially small and limited in population—less, at the highest figure, than any of the kingdoms of Europe. At its height, the territory of the Papal States did not exceed 16,000 square miles, and the population 3,125,000. In 1865, a little before its fall, its population had been reduced to 700,000.

7. It was, however, to be a very powerful horn, *"whose look was more stout than his fellows"* (Daniel 7:20). Need we say that

the Papacy has, at times, been the most powerful government in Europe, and, not only in assumption but in reality, has controlled the governments of the whole world?

8. It was to be an arrogant and pretentious horn, having "*a mouth speaking great things*" (Daniel 7:8). The Papacy has surely fulfilled all this. It has ever claimed the right to rule the kingdoms and consciences of people. It has made the mightiest potentates of Europe bow to its will and beg for its mercy. It forced the proudest emperor of Germany to do penance at its gates, barefoot on the icy ground, for three days at Canossa. There is not a nation within the limits of the Roman Empire that has not been humbled at its feet, and there is not a claim of arrogance and intolerance that it has not made. Its last assumption of infallibility has been the fitting crown of all preceding pretensions.

9. It was to be a blasphemous and impious power: "*He shall speak great words against the most High*" (Daniel 7:25). Dr. Young translates it thus: "*And words as an adversary of the Most High it doth speak*" (YLT). Surely, the Papacy has been the great adversary of the Most High. Surely, its words have been Satan's most hostile and effectual weapons for the perversion of truth and the subversion of souls.

10. It was to be a persecuting power: "*The same horn made war with the saints and prevailed against them*" (Daniel 7:21). He "*shall wear out the saints of the most High,…and they shall be given into his hand*" (Daniel 7:25). Papal Rome has butchered at least fifty million of the saints of God, tortured and tormented millions more, and "worn out" the people of God through all the long and weary centuries.

11. It was to "*think to change times and laws*" (Daniel 7:25). The Papacy has dictated the policy of European states, has been the great mistress of diplomacy and political intrigue, and has changed times by its great feasts and saints' days and the famous Gregorian calendar, which we owe to one of the popes.

12. It was to last *"a time and times and the dividing of time"* (Daniel 7:25)—that is, three and a half years of days, or 1,260 years.

From the various points from which the rise of the Papacy may be lawfully measured, a period of 1,260 years brings us to the most significant dates in the progress of its downfall. From the year AD 533, when Justinian established the supremacy of the pope over the churches of the world, 1,260 solar years bring us to 1793 and the horrors of the French Revolution, which, for a time, shattered and almost annihilated the papal power, as well as the governments of Europe.

From the years AD 607–610, when the emperor Phocas finally confirmed the supremacy of the popes, 1,260 years bring us to the last stage in the fall of the temporal powers—1867–1870—when, after his last infatuated claim of infallibility, the pope fell forever from his throne, and the little horn, as a political system, ceased to exist. At high noon on that eventful day, His Holiness had arranged to read the decree of infallibility amid brilliant mirrors, arranged to reflect the splendor of his person from every side of the gorgeous chamber. But when the hour came, the heavens were rent with thunder and tempest, and the sky overcast with clouds and storms. And before the day had closed, his fate was sealed, the fatal war between France and Germany was declared, and the course of events had begun that left him a prisoner in his palace and a fallen king of pride.

13. The destruction of this horn was not to be immediate but gradual. First, *"the Ancient of Days"* (Revelation 7:22), God the Father, in His providential government, was to come and sit in judgment upon it. Next, as describing a progressive picture, Daniel said, *"I beheld even till the beast was slain, and his body destroyed, and given to the burning flame"* (Daniel 7:11). Or, as Dr. Young translates it, *"I was seeing till that the beast is slain, and his body hath been destroyed, and given to the burning fire"* (YLT). And again,

in Daniel 7:26, the picture is still more vivid: *"The judgment shall sit, and they shall take away his dominion, to consume and to destroy it unto the end."* These are all successive steps. Dr. Young's *Literal Translation* brings out this feature yet more vividly: *"And the Judge is seated, and its dominion they cause to pass away, to cut off, and to destroy—unto the end"* (Daniel 7:26 YLT). It would seem that even after the dominion passes away from this horn, as it now has, the process of cutting off and destroying must still go on to the full consummation, as it is even now doing. Rome did not rise in a moment, and it will not fall in an hour. Its first deathblow was the Reformation, its second the French Revolution, its third the fall of the temporal power in 1870. It is going on to the end; and soon its still deeper and more persistent spiritual life will be smitten by *"the spirit of his mouth, and [destroyed] with the brightness of his coming"* (2 Thessalonians 2:8).

Paul's Picture

In 2 Thessalonians 2, the apostle Paul also gave us an inspired picture of this same system of evil:

> *That day shall not come, except there come a falling away first, and that man of sin be revealed....*   (2 Thessalonians 2:3)

> *The son of the destruction [Man of Sin]...is opposing and is raising himself up above all called God or worshipped, so that he in the sanctuary of God as God hath sat down, showing himself off that he is God....and now, what is keeping down ye have known, for his being revealed in his own time, for the secret of the lawlessness ["mystery of iniquity" KJV] doth already work, only he who is keeping down now [will hinder]— till he may be out of the way, and then shall be revealed the Lawless One, whom the Lord shall consume with the spirit of his mouth, and shall destroy with the manifestation of his*

presence, [him,] whose presence is according to the working of
the Adversary, in all power, and signs, and lying wonders, and
in all deceitfulness of the unrighteousness in those perishing,
because the love of the truth they did not receive for their being
saved ["that they might be saved" KJV].

(2 Thessalonians 2:3–4, 6–10 YLT[6])

In these passages, we are taught several additional facts concerning this same system of evil.

1. It was to be an apostasy, *"a falling away"* (2 Thessalonians 2:3). It was not to be a system of infidelity, paganism, or open devilishness; it was to come out of the very bosom of Christianity and was to be an apostate church. This is surely true of Romanism, which was once the pure church of Justin and Jerome and Clement and Augustine.

2. It was to be hindered in its development for a while by some other power, but was, even in the apostles' day, working in the church and was to break out without restraint when the hindering influence was removed. The spirit of Romanism—that is, ambition and ecclesiastical pride—was truly working in the apostolic church. Paul had to rebuke it at Corinth (see 1 Corinthians 1:10–4:21), and John found it so bitter and strong at Ephesus that he was even debarred from his own church by Diotrephes, "who loved the preeminence." (See 3 John 1:9.)

But it could never ripen into a Papacy as long as an emperor sat on Caesar's throne. A pope and a Caesar could not reign together. And, therefore, until Rome fell in AD 476, there was one *"keeping down"* (2 Thessalonians 3:6, 7 YLT). But with the fall of Rome, he was taken out of the way. And, very soon, the patriarchal government of the popes was recognized as the new sovereignty of Italy, and the way was prepared for the political supremacy of the Papacy.

3. It is described as a *"mystery of iniquity"* (2 Thessalonians 2:7) and a *"Lawless One"* (2 Thessalonians 2:8 YLT). Romanism is

a system of mysteries. It has seven sacraments, and secrets innumerable. Its confessional, its Jesuitical societies, its secret convocations and councils, and its policy of intrigue and diplomacy all justify this name given to it in Revelation: "*MYSTERY, BABYLON…*" (Revelation 17:5). And just as truly may it be called a system of lawlessness. Rome recognizes no authority above itself. It claims supremacy to human laws and lawgivers, and the right to make the laws and control the lawmakers. There is not a government on earth but has felt and resented this spirit, and this is the reason why it's priests and people have been driven out of China, Korea, Japan, and other countries; they were regarded as enemies of the state and emissaries of sedition. There is no divine law that papal indulgences and absolutions have not often put aside, and there is no form of iniquity that it has not harbored or concealed.

The wickedness, falsehood, duplicity, licentiousness, and corruption of the Papacy during the Middle Ages cannot easily be exaggerated. The Augustan age of Italian art was the age of most horrible priestly corruption, when the Italian Borgia rivaled the Roman Nero. The Protestant Reformation grew out of the abominations of papal indulgences, which were simply a selling of purity and righteousness for priestly and papal gain. The grosser revelations of the sins of the social and conventual system we do not enter upon, although these alone would sufficiently illustrate the fitness of the title "Man of Sin." It is enough to know that the life, spirit, and tendency of Romanism is unholy and iniquitous and that the races and countries where it has had its sway have become the most corrupt and immoral of all peoples.

4. It was to claim divine honors—sitting in the sanctuary of God, "*showing himself off that he is God*" (2 Thessalonians 2:4 YLT). The homage paid to the pope is idolatrous and divine. The names he uses in his decrees are blasphemous. The usual formula once was "our Lord God the Pope." The very character he assumes is that of the vicar, or actual representative, of Christ, clothed with

all His powers and dignities. And the last exhibition of his pretensions, the proclamation of his own infallibility amid gorgeous ceremonies, was indeed a literal *"showing himself off that he is God."* There is not one expression here too strong for the naked and repeated facts of ecclesiastical history.

5. His coming is declared to be *"after the working of Satan with all power and signs and lying wonders, and with all deceivableness of unrighteousness"* (2 Thessalonians 2:9–10). If ever the devil had a masterpiece, it is the Papacy. His one desire ever has been to mimic God, and here He has had a splendid counterfeit. Neither have there been lacking the greatest power and the most arresting and remarkable signs of supernatural origin. The miracles of the Papacy have been of two classes. Some of them are *"lying wonders,"* mere skillful pretensions. But some have been the results of real satanic power and actual signs of supernatural working, as much as the predicted miracles of spiritualism. And then there is also *"all deceivableness of unrighteousness"*—the evil that is made to look like good, the lie that is justified in the interests of the church, the perversion of Scripture, the duplicity of Jesuitism, and the false principles that underlie the whole life it teaches.

6. Its judgment is to come from two sources. The first is *"the spirit of his mouth"* (2 Thessalonians 2:8). Surely, this denotes the Word of God; and, truly, this is the weapon with which He has been destroying Rome since the liberation of the Bible by Wycliffe five hundred years ago. There is a fine old cartoon in one of Wycliffe's Bibles. A little fire has broken out in the midst of a company of cardinals and priests. It is burning inside the covers of a Bible. It is spreading rapidly. They all gather around it and try to blow it out. There is His Holiness, blowing till his cheeks are bursting, as well as scores of puffing priests and bishops. But the more they blow, the more it burns, until, at last, they are compelled to fly to escape its consuming flame. So has the Bible been consuming Rome; and, with a true instinct, Rome has dreaded and suppressed the Bible.

7. But the final blow is to come from *"the brightness of his coming"* (2 Thessalonians 2:8), which will consume and finally extinguish this mystery of sin. For that we wait. The first process has been long in progress; the last is near.

John's Picture

In John's vision, the system of evil is chiefly described in the thirteenth, seventeenth, and eighteenth chapters of Revelation.

1. It is described as a wild beast *"whose deadly wound was healed"* (Revelation 13:12). Revelation 13 begins with a picture of the same wild beast that Daniel saw in his fourth vision—the Roman beast with its ten horns. But here it is seen with seven heads (see Revelation 13:1), and the seventh of these is the Papacy, the same power that in Daniel's vision was seen as a little horn, but that really exercises all the power of the beast itself, and is in fact called *"the beast"* in Daniel 7:11. Here it is called a "head," one of the seven heads of this monstrous beast. Six other heads had preceded it. These were the six different forms of government under which Rome has existed: kings, consuls, dictators, decemvirs, tribunes, and emperors. The angel declared to Saint John that five of these heads had fallen; and one, the empire, was in existence at the time of the vision. The seventh had *"not yet come"* (Revelation 17:19), and when it did, it must continue for *"a little time"* (Revelation 17:19 YLT), that is, a considerable time. That was tantamount to saying, "It will last awhile when it comes."

John said that he saw one of these heads wounded to death. That refers to the fall of the empire under Romulus Augustulus in the year 476. Then, indeed, it seemed as if the beast had received its deathblow. But his *"deadly wound was healed."* He had vitality enough in him to put forth another head, and it gave to the whole body a life and power that it had never possessed before.

How wonderfully this describes the rise of the Papacy out of the ruins of imperial Rome, and the revival it brought to the city, which was about to sink into obscurity and ruins. Even Gibbon, the profane and infidel historian, described this event almost like an interpreter of prophecy:

> Like Thebes, or Babylon, or Carthage, the name of Rome might have been erased from the earth, if the city had not been animated by a vital principle, which again restored her to honor and dominion.[7]

> The empire having been overthrown, unless God had raised up the *Pontificate*, Rome, resuscitated and restored by none, would have become uninhabitable, and been a most foul habitation thenceforward of cattle. But in the Pontificate it revived as with a *second birth*.[8]

And so, once more, the wild beast revived in another form. Rome became for twelve centuries the center and metropolis of the world, *"and all the world wondered after the beast"* (Revelation 13:3).

2. It is described later in the same chapter, under a second image, as *"another beast…*[with] *two horns like a lamb, and he spake as a dragon"* (Revelation 13:11). This denotes another side of the Papacy, namely, its ecclesiastical and spiritual organization. The first beast represents its political and temporal power; the second its ecclesiastical. It is really two systems. It is both a church and a state; or, rather, it was until 1870. It had a political existence as real as France or Germany, and much more pretentious. And it had an ecclesiastical system quite independent of its political government, which was able to go on even if that were suspended, as indeed it has been going on since 1870. Now, this is the system represented by the two-horned lamb, with the dragon tongue—innocent looking as a lamb but speaking the devil's words in its bulls and decretals, its indulgences, interdicts, and anathemas.

3. These two phases and aspects of this system are combined in the picture of Revelation 17, in which the spiritual and ecclesiastical aspect of the Papacy is represented as an abandoned woman, while the temporal power is denoted by the beast on which she rides. This is the apostate church, supported by the arm and sword of earthly power, trampling down the consciences and rights and lives of all who oppose her despotic will.

Many times in Scripture, a woman is used as a type of evil. The prototype of this same evil power was the ancient Jezebel of Samaria. In Zechariah, the emblem of corruption is a woman, sitting in an ephah and carried forth to Babylon. (See Zechariah 5:7–11.) In the parable of the leaven, it is a woman who prefigures the spirit of corruption there symbolized. (See, for example, Matthew 13:33.) John wondered at this woman because, just before this, he had seen the church as a woman clothed with the sun. (See Revelation 12.) Alas, that so soon the bride of Christ should seem like a harlot!

4. Again, in Revelation 17, and more fully in Revelation 18, the same system of evil is described by yet another name: "*Babylon,*" or "*Mystery, Babylon…*". That is, not the real Babylon but the mystical one, corresponding in spirit and destiny—in pride, profligacy, and destiny—to the ancient queen of empires. This name may refer particularly to the city of Rome, as much as to the system of Romanism. We know this name was given to it by the early fathers, and even Peter, in writing his epistle from "Babylon," is thought by many to have really meant Rome. (See 1 Peter 5:13.) In the eighteenth chapter, the fall of Babylon probably involves the destruction of the city of Rome.

5. The next feature of this system of evil is universal dominion. "*Power was given him over all kindreds, and tongues, and nations*" (Revelation 13:7). During the Middle Ages, the power of Rome was universal, at least so far as the world was under the sway of any European state.

6. It was to be a blasphemous power. (See Revelation 13:1, 5–6; 17:3.) We cannot better interpret this than by quoting the following reference to the names and claims of the Roman pontiff at various periods in the past:

> He claims a homage which even rivals that of Jehovah. Some of the titles which have been given to him are truly awful. Christopher Marcellus, in the fourth session of the fifth Lateran Council, called Pope Julius II *another God upon earth*. In the sixth session of the same council, Leo X was called by Simon Bengnius *the Saviour that was to come*; and the same Pope, in the next session of that council, was called *King of kings*.

7. It was to be worshipped. (See, for example, Revelation 13:4, 8.) The word *"worship"* here applied both to the beast and the dragon. This worship of the beast was really a worship of the dragon. Papal worship is, therefore, devil worship. The word *"worshipped"* here literally means "kissed." The method of papal worship is to kiss the big toe. And in Saint Peter's Basilica in Rome, the bronze statue said to represent Saint Peter has had more than half its toe literally kissed away. To make the description still more literal, it is said that this statue is not Saint Peter at all but just an old heathen Jupiter found at Rome and dedicated to the great apostle. If this is so, then their worship is truly to the dragon, for all the gods of Greece and Rome were literally symbols of demon powers.

8. He was to do *"great wonders"* and to deceive those who dwelt on earth by those miracles that he would have power to do. (See Revelation 13:13.) This describes the miraculous claims of Romanism and the false, deceptive character of some, as well as the undoubted supernatural reality of others.

9. He was to call down fire from heaven. (See Revelation 13:13.) This might well describe the anathemas of the popes that call fire down from heaven on all who provoke them.

10. He was to control the very buying and selling of all who refused his authority. (See Revelation 13:16–17.) How exactly this describes a papal *interdict*, which the pontiffs sometimes passed on refractory subjects, completely cutting them off from all human fellowship, and forbidding all persons to transact business with them.

11. The beast is denoted by a numerical name—666. (See Revelation 13:18.) While there have been innumerable guesses as to the meaning of this mystical number, no interpretation seems more reasonable than that of Irenaeus, the Christian father: the numerical value of each letter of the word *Lateinos*, when added together, equals the number 666. *Lateinos* means "Latin," and it is especially applicable to Romanism, which is called Latin Christianity, and which, since the year 663, has made the Latin language the vehicle of its teaching.

12. The papal woman is clothed in scarlet, and the beast she rides is also scarlet. (See Revelation 17:3–4.) We need not say that this is the chosen color of Rome, the Pontiffs' and the Bishops' robes, and all the great processions and fetes, making scarlet the distinctively papal color. It would seem as if the Lord had ordered that Rome should establish her own identity by her very face.

13. She was *"decked with…precious stones"* (Revelation 17:4; 18:16). Who has not wondered at the countless treasures of Roman altars? Let anyone go through the famous Basilica of Saint Paul Outside the Walls and look at the altars presented by various European sovereigns, flashing with the splendors of jasper and sardonyx, and it will be strange if he does not leave with a sense of worldly show such as the most extravagant earthly entertainment could not rival, and with the thought of how much better these things could serve the Master if converted into Bibles and scattered throughout the world.

14. She was represented as a harlot committing fornication with the kings of the earth. (See Revelation 17:1–2.) The idea,

of course, is the unholy union of the papal church and the governments of earth. This has been the story of European politics for twelve centuries. The Papacy has always leaned upon the sword. She obtained her first decrees of universal supremacy from Roman emperors; her grants of territory came from Pepin and Charlemagne and the Princess Matilda; her butcheries of Protestants were carried out by the hands of the Duke of Alva and the Catholic powers of Europe. Her last years were upheld by the bayonets of France and Austria, and her present attempt is to get control of the democracies of Europe and America.

15. She is represented as holding in her hand *"a golden cup... full of abominations"* (Revelation 17:4). The very seal of Rome is a woman holding in her hand a golden cup with the inscription *Sedet super universum*.[9]

16. She is to be first supported by the kings of the earth and then despoiled by them. *"These shall hate the whore, and shall make her desolate and naked, and shall eat her flesh, and burn her with fire"* (Revelation 17:16). This is one of the most remarkable fulfillments of prophecy. The world has witnessed just this spectacle for nearly one hundred years. France, the eldest son of the Papacy, was the first to turn upon her. The French Revolution struck her the first terrible blow, and then Napoleon finished it, capturing and deposing the pope himself. Then Italy finished what France began. Portugal has since followed suit. And, today, Cardinal Manning truly says there is not a nation to stand up for the rights of the Church.

17. The same picture that Daniel gave marks her as a persecuting power. She was *"drunken with the blood of the saints, and with the blood of the martyrs of Jesus"* (Revelation 17:6).

18. The same duration is also assigned as was given by Daniel: *"Power was given unto him to continue forty and two months"* (Revelation 13:5), that is, 1,260 years.

19. The fall of Rome is described in the eighteenth chapter. This has not yet come. It would seem to indicate some sudden and appalling catastrophe coming *"in one hour"* (Revelation 18:10, 17, 19) and engulfing the city of ages in a ruin like Sodom and Gomorrah. Ever since the days of the fathers, it has been supposed that this will come through some great natural convulsion, and that Rome will go to its doom amid earthquake shock and fearful eruptions of fire and brimstone.

20. But before this comes, it may yet have much to develop. Out of its mouth, as well as the mouth of the dragon and the false prophet, are to go (and are going) *"three unclean spirits like frogs…. For they are the spirits of devils, working miracles"* (Revelation 16:13–14). These unclean spirits are to gather the kings of the earth to the last battle of the present age—the day of Armageddon. (See Revelation 16:14.)

21. It is to grow more distinctly and manifestly evil to the close. And its last head will be the devil himself. When Romanism falls, then Satan, in person, is to be the head of the old Roman beast, leading the powers of earth once more against the Lamb. *"The beast that was and is not, even he is the eighth, and is of the seven, and goeth into perdition"* (Revelation 17:11).

This, then, is the divine picture of the great apostasy. Today, she is making her last desperate struggle. Let us not be deceived. Her kingdom is gone, but her life is not dead. Innumerable facts show her vitality. She is not going to be converted but consumed. But there is a remnant in her bosom that God is calling forth. And, preparatory to the end, our ministry is to send forth the heralds of the gospel among all her benighted votaries and cry, *"Come out of her, my people, that ye be not partakers of her sins, and that ye receive not of her plagues"* (Revelation 18:4).

CHAPTER SIX

THE FALSE PROPHET

*"And out of one of them came forth a little horn, which
waxed exceeding great, toward the south, and toward the
east, and toward the pleasant land. And it waxed great, even
to the host of heaven; and it cast down some of the host and
of the stars to the ground, and stamped upon them....And by
him the daily sacrifice was taken away, and the place of the
sanctuary was cast down. And an host was given him against
the daily sacrifice by reason of transgression, and it cast down
the truth to the ground; and it practised, and prospered."*
—Daniel 8:9–12

We have seen that the seventh chapter of Daniel describes
a little horn that was to rise in the west and become the most
prominent figure in the last ages of Christendom. In the very next
chapter, however, Daniel describes another little horn that was to
rise in the east, out of the subdivisions of the Greek Empire, and
become the most prominent figure in the subsequent history of the
Jewish people. It is to this that we now turn our attention.

It is noteworthy that the preceding chapters of Daniel, from the second to the seventh, are written in Chaldee; the picture of the world is written in the world's language. But from the eighth chapter, where the powers that were to deal with the Jews are brought before us, the Hebrew language is employed.

This vision describes the fall of the Persian Empire before the Macedonian Empire, the breaking asunder of Alexander himself, and the rise of four horns to succeed him. These four horns are the four sections into which Alexander's empire was divided.

The four sections were Central Asia, Greece, Egypt, and Syria. Out of one of these, the little horn was to arise. That one was Syria. Its ancient kings, especially Antiochus Epiphanes, fulfilled, in the most literal manner, as prototypes, all that is here predicted about the little horn—so far as he could in that early day. But we are distinctly told in the close of the vision that it is *"for many days"* (Daniel 8:26) and that it reaches out even to 2,300 years (see Daniel 8:14). Therefore, it could not have been fulfilled by Antiochus, except in anticipation, just as the destruction of Jerusalem was a foreshadowing of the second coming of Christ.

The Rise and Progress of Islamic Power

Its complete fulfillment, we believe, is to be found only in the rise and progress of that widespread and long-continued system of iniquity and satanic policy that has overspread the Eastern world for centuries, just as Romanism has the West. We mean Islam. Let us look at the points of resemblance, as in the case of the other horn.

1. It was to rise out of one of the horns of Alexander's divided kingdom. In one sense, Islam sways the whole region that came out of Alexander's empire. Greece, Egypt, Syria, and Central Asia have all been held by its despotic hand for many centuries, and its capital, Constantinople [Istanbul], was the last seat of the Greek

Empire. But it seems more natural to think of it as the successor of the ancient Syrian kings, in the sovereignty of Syria and Palestine. One of the very first conquests of the Muslims was Damascus, and they may be more truly called the successors of the Syrian kings and the Greek Empire than any power on earth today.

2. It was to be *"a little horn"* (Daniel 8:9). Islam originated in Arabia. And when Muhammad began his career, Arabia was the last land on earth to seem likely to subdue one-half of the world. There was scarcely a single independent prince in all the land. And even yet, Arabia is a thinly populated and unimportant country, quite as much a little horn as the Papal States of Italy.

3. It was to wax exceeding great *"toward the south, and toward the east, and toward the pleasant land"* (Daniel 8:9). And these were exactly the directions of Muslim aggression. First, it conquered Arabia; then, it spread east toward Central Asia, subjugating Persia, Assyria, Babylonia, and Syria, and afterward Palestine and Egypt. As centuries rolled on, its vast dominion became much wider, reaching over northern Africa, southern Europe, India, and much of southern and eastern Asia. It was indeed *"exceeding great"* (Daniel 8:9), and so tremendous was its power and prestige that only the hand of God and the courage of Charles Martel[10] saved the whole of Europe from being overrun.

4. Its spirit is represented under the figure of *"a king of fierce countenance"* (Daniel 8:23). And so Islam ever has been as cruel as the grave. Its conquests were inexorable, and its awful alternative was the Koran or the sword. Its soldiers have been called

> That cruel, murderous crew,
> To carnage and the Koran given;
> Who think through unbelievers' blood
> Lies the securest path to heaven.[11]

5. It was to attack Christianity, to magnify itself against the host of heaven and to cast some of the stars down to the ground.

(See Daniel 8:10.) This was terribly fulfilled in the first conquests of the Muslims. Their opponents were chiefly the Eastern Christians and the armies of the Greek Empire. Their victims received no quarter except by embracing the Koran, and multitudes of people and pastors perished in the awful tempest. Syria, Palestine, Persia, Asia Minor, and North Africa were the very seats of Eastern Christianity, yet, in a generation, Christianity was almost wholly obliterated from all these regions. Today, we find only a few scattered Nestorians, Armenians, and Copts, who have almost forgotten the very elements of apostolic Christianity. Thus, we can realize how complete has been the desolation of this scourge.

6. It was to be *"by reason of transgression"* (Daniel 8:12) that God would thus allow His cause and His people to be spoiled and scourged. Eastern Christianity had become as thoroughly corrupt as the Roman Papacy. Image worship filled all the Greek churches, and Muhammad considered himself a real purifier of religion and a destroyer of idolatry. The latter he surely was, although he brought in a more terrible substitute.

7. It was especially to desolate the Holy Land—to take away the daily sacrifice, to tread down the place of the sanctuary (see Daniel 8:11–12), and to set up the abomination of desolation (see Daniel 8:13; Matthew 24:15; Mark 13:14). The word *sacrifice* is not in the original Hebrew. It is simply "the daily," or "the continual," and it may refer to worship as much as to sacrifice. We know that in the year AD 637, Omar captured Jerusalem and immediately set up the Mosque of Omar on the site of Solomon's Temple. The place of the sanctuary was indeed cast down, and the old bishop went out of the city crying, "The abomination of desolation is set up." Since that time, for twelve hundred years, the Muslims have been the desolators of Jerusalem and Judea. It was to recover the city of Jerusalem from this humiliation that the Crusades were undertaken. But Islam still treads down the ancient land, and it will until the seed of Abraham inherits it again.

8. This power was to *"be broken without hand"* (Daniel 8:25). And so the Muslim power has been breaking for two hundred years by the unseen hand of God, and all the fostering care of Europe cannot much longer keep Islam alive.

9. The time that should elapse from the initial date until the end of its oppression and the restoration of Jerusalem was to be 2,300 years. The natural starting point of this date is the decree of Artaxerxes to restore and rebuild Jerusalem, the same point from which the seventy weeks are dated. Those are said to be cut off from the larger period of 2,300 years. That was 457 BC. From that point, 2,300 years bring us to 1844, the very date when, after more than a century of humiliation and disaster, Turkey was compelled to pass the great Edict of Toleration, revoking the law that prohibited a Turkish subject from embracing Christianity under pain of death. It was the most marked stage in the destruction of the desolator, and it has been followed ever since by successive blows and judgments clearly foreshadowing the end of its power.

The Spiritual Strength of Islamic Power

The fall of Turkey does not involve the destruction of Islam any more than the fall of the temporal power has killed Romanism. Islam, as a system, is still intensely alive. From its great university in Cairo, ten thousand students are ever going out as evangelists of Islam. It holds 175 million of the human race yet under its thrall, and they are almost inaccessible to the light. Its followers are rapidly increasing every year. It will not be fully destroyed until the coming of Christ. Then, the beast and the false prophet will both be cast into the lake of fire.

CHAPTER SEVEN

THE LAST DEVELOPMENT OF ANTICHRIST

In the closing stages of human history, will there be an appearance of a personal antichrist, or are all the predictions of Scripture fulfilled in the great apostasies that we have already so fully described?

Too much has been made of the personal description of the Man of Sin, and it is too hastily assumed from this description that he must be an individual man. The argument is not as forcible as it seems. Regarding the vision of Nebuchadnezzar, Daniel declared, in interpreting it to the king, *"Thou art this head of gold"* (Daniel 2:38). A literal interpretation would require that the vision must be fulfilled in the personal history of the king himself. We know, however, that it was fulfilled in the kingdom of Babylon, of which he was the head and representative. The individual ever passes; the office remains. Theoretically, the king never dies, although the individual kings are constantly changing. In this sense, then, the *"man of sin"* (2 Thessalonians 2:3) may well represent a great system of evil, the system that is described, in the same passage, as *"the mystery of iniquity"* (2 Thessalonians 2:7).

And yet, there is nothing to forbid a double interpretation of these prophecies—first, as a system of evil lasting through long centuries; and, second, as one great leader in whom the whole system and perhaps all other systems of evil will be headed up for the final conflict. This idea is strongly suggested, if not distinctly taught, in the remarkable passage in the sixteenth chapter of the book of Revelation, where *"three unclean spirits like frogs"* (Revelation 16:13) are represented as going forth from the three great leaders of the forces of evil—the dragon, the beast, and the false prophet—to gather the world of the ungodly for the last great conflict with Christ. Here it is evident that more than one system of evil is represented. Indeed, it is certain from the context that this is a combination of all the forms of existing evil, a great confederacy of opposition to the Lord and His servants. For such a combination, there must certainly be a common leader—a leader of exceptional brilliance and capacity. This will require the supreme genius of human history, the great superman, of whom all the pharaohs, Caesars, Alexanders, and Napoleons have been the prototypes.

Who Will the "Last Antichrist" Be?

The various prophecies in Daniel, 2 Thessalonians, and Revelation throw some extraordinary light on the genius and ability of this personality. Indeed, it is difficult to believe that any mere human being can wholly fulfill the description. He is to be at once a great politician, a despotic ruler, and a supreme religious leader—combining the diplomacy, intellectual culture, ecclesiastical authority, and military genius of the race. It would seem from the description given in Revelation 13 that he is also to be the head of all industrial and commercial corporations and combinations, that all business is to be carried on under direct license from him, and that all religious worship is to be absolutely under his control and actually offered personally to him.

We are not left without a very clear intimation of who this awful and mysterious personality will really be. In Revelation 17:8–11, we have a remarkable description of the great system of evil that has cursed the world through the ages, down to its very latest development. The description is of a wild beast with seven heads and ten horns. We have already seen these seven heads in the previous visions. The latest of them was shown to be that great system of iniquity that formed the subject of our last chapter. But here, an eighth head is introduced that we have not seen before. It would appear, therefore, that after the seventh wicked head has accomplished its evil work, and just before its final destruction, this eighth head is to appear and become the leader of all the forces of evil that are now culminating in the last hours of time.

Furthermore, this last head is described as *"of the seven"* (Revelation 17:11). That is, he has been intimately identified with each of the previous heads, although hitherto out of sight and working as a silent partner through his visible earthly representatives. Now, however, he openly assumes the leadership of his forces and gathers up, in this final combination that we have already described, all the elements of lawlessness and antagonism to God that had been his own subtle and devilish work throughout the ages. In short, this last leader is none other than Satan himself, who now appears upon the scene openly and visibly as the last Antichrist.

His identification is perfectly certain from the description given of him: "[He] *shall ascend out of the bottomless pit, and go into perdition*" (Revelation 17:8). There is only one who answers to this description. It is that one who is described repeatedly as *"the dragon"* and *"that old serpent, which is the Devil, and Satan"* (Revelation 12:9, 20:2). People may laugh at the idea of a personal devil as much as they like, and the very fact that they do laugh so loud is the best evidence of his skill and success, for his strategy is to hide his personality and persuade people that either there never was a devil or that the devil is dead. But, someday, they will be disillusioned. He will throw off his disguise and, probably in human form, will appear in his true colors and defy the Almighty Himself.

The great ambition of the evil one has always been to mimic God and to pose as the object of human homage, worship, and obedience. There is nothing incredible in the idea that he should seek to copy the Lord Jesus Christ, even in His incarnation. It would indeed be a piece of splendid strategy for him to manifest himself in the flesh, even as the Lord Jesus has been manifest, and to play the part of the counterfeit and rival of the Lamb of God to the very end of the chapter. Doubtless, he will still seek to hide his satanic character and will seem to people to be the most wonderful and brilliant human genius that has ever represented the race of Adam. But behind him will be the super-resources of the great archangel of the underworld, that mighty being whom the Scriptures uniformly describe as less only than God Himself.

What an hour of darkness and crisis that last hour of the present dispensation will indeed be. The conflict is described in Revelation 17:13–14: "*These have one mind, and shall give their power and strength unto the beast. These shall make war with the Lamb, and the Lamb shall overcome them: for He is Lord of lords and King of kings.*" Chapters 19 and 20 of Revelation continue this dramatic and awful picture:

> *And I saw the beast, and the kings of the earth, and their armies, gathered together to make war against him that sat on the horse, and against his army. And the beast was taken, and with him the false prophet that wrought miracles before him, with which he deceived them that had received the mark of the beast, and them that worshipped his image. These both were cast alive into a lake of fire burning with brimstone....*

*And I saw an angel come down from heaven, having the key of
the bottomless pit and a great chain in his hand. And he laid
hold on the dragon, that old serpent, which is the Devil, and
Satan, and bound him a thousand years, and cast him into the
bottomless pit, and shut him up, and set a seal upon him, that
he should deceive the nations no more, till the thousand years
should be fulfilled: and after that he must be loosed a little
season.* (Revelation 19:19–20; 20:1–3)

Thus will end, for a thousand years, at least, the tragedy of
time. How solemnly things are heading up for these final developments and this great consummation.

The Advent of the "Superman"

A volume has recently been published in England and America,
by Mr. Philip Mauro, with the striking title *The Number of Man*.
In this work, the author develops, with great ingenuity and intel-
ligence, the theory that all the political, social, religious, economic,
and intellectual conditions of our day are converging to one great
final combination or corporation, which will control the politics,
the business, and the religion of the world at no distant date and
fulfill literally the picture given in Revelation 13.

The author forcibly points out that this is the age of combinations, and that everything is moving toward vast consolidations
of capital, labor, and even religious work. Moreover, these various individual combinations are moving closer together toward
a general corporation of corporations, the great Trust of Trusts.
He shows forcibly and truly how socialism is aiming to develop
a religious element and is proclaiming the religion of humanity.
In line with this, the new theologies of Mr. Campbell in England
and Newman Smythe and Dr. Gordon in America are claiming
kinship with socialism and offering to it a new theological creed,

upon which all who believe in the religion of humanity can join. He shows how this movement has sprung up in Roman Catholic countries under the name of Modernism, which is essentially one with the socialistic and liberal movement in the churches. All these movements unite in demanding that business should be under the control of the state, and that the state should have a religious basis along the broad lines already indicated.

Furthermore, it is easy to see that the religious trend today is steadily toward liberalism, compromise, union, fraternity, universalism—the putting down of all the bars and the setting up of a platform so wide that the Protestant, the Roman Catholic, the Jew, and the Buddhist will feel equally at home, provided only that they are sincere in what they believe.

Surely, the great arch-leader has his organization almost ready for his personal advent. The great spectacle of the "solidarity of man" will soon be followed by the advent of the superman. And when we remember that he is to be no less than Satan himself, the program is complete, and the world's most stupendous hour is at hand.

CHAPTER EIGHT

THE GREAT TRIBULATION

"Because thou hast kept the word of my patience, I also will keep thee from the hour of temptation [tribulation], which shall come upon all the world, to try them that dwell upon the earth. Behold, I come quickly: hold that fast which thou hast, that no man take thy crown."
—Revelation 3:10–11

"Watch ye therefore, and pray always, that ye may be counted worthy to escape all these things that shall come to pass, and to stand before the Son of man."
—Luke 21:36

There looms large and dark in the vista of prophecy a dreadful cloud upon the future of this world.

Earth, what a sorrow lies before thee,
None like it in the shadowy past;

The sharpest throe that ever tore thee,
E'en tho' the briefest and the last![12]

Isaiah asked the watchman, "*What of the night?*" (Isaiah 21:11), and the answer came, "*The morning cometh, and also the night*" (Isaiah 21:12). The last shadows blot out the dawn. Jeremiah cried, "*Alas! for that day is great, so that none is like it: it is even the time of Jacob's trouble*" (Jeremiah 30:7). And Jesus Christ told us in His Olivet discourse, "*Then shall be great tribulation, such as was not since the beginning of the world to this time, no, nor ever shall be. And except those days should be shortened, there should no flesh be saved: but for the elect's sake those days shall be shortened*" (Matthew 24:21–22).

Israel's Day of Trouble

This dreadful hour of sorrow is to be especially severe upon Israel. We have already quoted Jeremiah's prophecy of Jacob's trouble, but the prophet added, "*…he shall be saved out of it*" (Jeremiah 30:7). Daniel, in the last chapter of his book, reached the following closing vision of the Christian age:

> *There shall be a time of trouble, such as never was since there was a nation even to that same time: and at that time thy people shall be delivered, every one that shall be found written in the book.* (Daniel 12:1)

That this time is the distant future is revealed by the next verse: "*Many of them that sleep in the dust of the earth shall awake*" (Daniel 12:2).

Zechariah more fully pictures this catastrophe, this furnace worse than the Egyptian bondage:

> *And it shall come to pass, that in all the land, saith the LORD, two parts therein shall be cut off and die; but the third shall*

be left therein. And I will bring the third part through the fire, and will refine them as silver is refined, and will try them as gold is tried: they shall call on my name, and I will hear them: I will say, It is my people: and they shall say, The LORD is my God.…I will gather all nations against Jerusalem to battle; and the city shall be taken, and the houses rifled, and the women ravished; and half of the city shall go forth into captivity, and the residue of the people shall not be cut off from the city. Then shall the LORD go forth, and fight against those nations, as when he fought in the day of battle. And his feet shall stand in that day upon the mount of Olives.

(Zechariah 13:8–9; 14:2–4)

Distress of Nations

It will be a day of trouble not only for Israel, but for all the nations. In Luke's report of the Olivet address, we have this full account of the tribulation: "*There shall be…upon the earth distress of nations*" (Luke 21:25). "*Distress*" here is an extremely intense word. It is more than distress. It is desperate distress, unparalleled distress, distress that leaves men at their wit's end, so that, as John told us in the vision of the apocalypse, "*In those days shall men seek death, and shall not find it*" (Revelation 9:6).

Distress of nations, with perplexity; the sea and the waves roaring; men's hearts failing them for fear, and for looking after those things which are coming upon the earth: for the powers of heaven shall be shaken. (Luke 21:25–26)

We hear the mutterings already, the volcanic forces that are underlying our social, industrial, and political life, and that might easily break forth at any moment but for the restraining providences that will be removed in that tribulation time.

Causes of the Coming Tribulation

Let us look briefly at some of the causes of this dread condition of things that is coming upon the earth.

1. The first cause is the natural ripening of sin. It will be the human heart in its corruption and depravity, and with all the added forces of modern development and culture, reaching the highest possibilities of wickedness and misery. We have just such a picture as this in Revelation 14:18—this ripening of the vine of earth: *"Thrust in thy sharp sickle, and gather the clusters of the vine of the earth; for her grapes are fully ripe."*

We have a little account of the ripening of humanity's unrestrained physical life in the early chapters of the Bible. At the beginning of Genesis, we read that *"there were giants in the earth in those days"* (Genesis 6:4). People developed the species by high breeding until, through physical development, such as scientists are telling us about today, they reached a condition of the very highest physical perfection. The women, we are told, were beautiful women. The believers of that day—the descendants of the godly Seth— regardless of God's separating line, mingled with the world and *"took them wives of all which they chose"* (Genesis 6:2). They married anyone they wanted to. They married without any thought of what God wanted, and thus they mingled the seed, contrary to God's prohibition. They developed a remarkable race of physical perfection, the highest types perhaps that humanity had developed, even in that age when human life was still long and when the seeds of death had not fully wrought their fruit of mortality.

But what was the result? A race so morally corrupt that the earth was filled with violence, and God had to send a deluge to wash away the pollution of their sins and crimes. (See Genesis 6–7.) A little later, human wickedness developed into the fearful and unnatural vices of *"the cities of the plain,"* and God once more had to burn out the stench of human wickedness, this time by a rain of fire. (See Genesis 19:1–29.)

The Lord Jesus has told us that moral conditions on earth at the time of His coming will be as in the days of Noah and Lot. (See, for example, Luke 17:26–30.) Human nature will have reached not only its perfect physical development but also its highest intellectual and social culture; and humanity's capacity for wickedness will be at its maximum. The two special features suggested by the days of Noah and the days of Lot in the moral picture are violence and lust. We can already see the beginnings of these last developments in the lawlessness of our own age and the breaking away of modern society from all restraint in self-indulgence. We need only imagine these conditions at their height, and earth would again be an inferno like the scene that the angels met that awful night when they came down to the house of Lot to investigate the wickedness of Sodom.

2. It will be the result of satanic power. The tribulation time will be Satan's *"hour, and...power of darkness"* (Luke 22:53).

> *And I saw three unclean spirits like frogs come out of the mouth of the dragon, and out of the mouth of the beast, and out of the mouth of the false prophet. For they are the spirits of devils, working miracles, which go forth unto the kings of the earth and of the whole world, to gather them to the battle of that great day of God Almighty.*   (Revelation 16:13–14)

The frog suggests the night, and this will be the Night of the Ages. The frog suggests the pestilential swamp, and earth will be one deadly quagmire of moral putridity. The frog speaks with a dismal croak, and the note of infidelity, materialism, spiritualism, and atheism is one of gloom, depression, and despair.

These three spirits are already beginning their dire work. The unclean spirit from the mouth of the dragon may well be recognized in the croakings of spiritualism. The frog from the mouth of the beast is busy in the swamp of socialism and anarchy. And the emissary of the false prophet is abroad in the varied forms of present fanaticism, materialism, Christian Science, Theosophy, and even Religious Liberalism. Let all these things have unrestricted sway, and we will already be in the great tribulation.

4. The tribulation period will be the time when antichrist will reign, and all the world will be under the arbitrary and cruel sway of the last and worst form of human government, represented by the beast. Think for a moment of the condition of the Jews today in Russia under that oppressive government. Make it universal, and earth would be a hell. Think of the excesses of socialism, as well as of the dynamiter and the anarchist, and what more would be needed to constitute the great tribulation? Think of a world where no person could buy or sell or transact any kind of business without a license from this superman, as will be the case when the prophecy of Revelation 13:15–17 is fulfilled. Who would wish to live on earth in such an evil time?

4. The tribulation will be the time of God's particular judgments upon this wicked world. Many believe that the trumpet woes of Revelation 8 belong to this period. Certainly, the awful picture of Revelation 14:19–20 belongs to this time:

> And the angel thrust in his sickle into the earth, and gathered the vine of the earth, and cast it into the great winepress of the wrath of God. And the winepress was trodden without the city, and blood came out of the winepress, even unto the horse bridles, by the space of a thousand and six hundred furlongs.

At last will come the final conflict:

> And he gathered them together into a place called in the Hebrew tongue Armageddon....And I saw the beast, and the kings of the earth, and their armies, gathered together to make war against him that sat on the horse, and against his army. And the beast was taken, and with him the false prophet that

*wrought miracles before him....These both were cast alive into
a lake of fire burning with brimstone.*

(Revelation 16:16; 19:19–20)

5. The tribulation will be a time when the restraints of religion
will be withdrawn from the world—the church will *"be caught up...
to meet the Lord in the air"* (1 Thessalonians 4:17), and human society will be without the presence and restraining influence of the
followers of Christ. What a dreadful world this will be when the
atmosphere of faith and love and prayer is at last withdrawn, and the
awful shadow of the dragon's wing rests like a pall of despair upon
every human heart. God grant that we may escape that dreadful day.

The period of the great tribulation appears to be fixed by the
words of Christ:

> *Immediately after the tribulation of those days shall the sun be
> darkened, and the moon shall not give her light, and the stars
> shall fall from heaven, and the powers of the heavens shall be
> shaken: and then shall appear the sign of the Son of man in
> heaven: and then shall all the tribes of the earth mourn, and
> they shall see the Son of man coming in the clouds of heaven
> with power and great glory.* (Matthew 24:29–30)

The tribulation, therefore, will follow the *parousia* of the Son
of Man, when His church will be withdrawn to meet Him in the
air, and when the holy dead will be united with them in the first
resurrection; and, it will precede the public manifestation of the
Lord Jesus Christ in His glorious epiphany.

How Will We Escape?

Finally, how will we escape this awful day? We cannot do
better than to read the Lord's last message in the third chapter of
Revelation:

Because thou hast kept the word of my patience, I also will keep thee from the hour of temptation, which shall come upon all the world, to try them that dwell upon the earth. Behold, I come quickly: hold that fast which thou hast, that no man take thy crown.   (Revelation 3:10–11)

Those who keep the word of His patience, who believe His word and live it, will therefore be numbered with His waiting bride and will be saved from this awful catastrophe.

What are these which are arrayed in white robes? and whence came they? And I said unto him, Sir, thou knowest. And he said to me, These are they which came out of great tribulation, and have washed their robes, and made them white in the blood of the Lamb.   (Revelation 7:13–14)

In the Greek, a definite article is included, as follows: "*These are they which came out of* [the] *great tribulation.*" They escape it; they are caught up in Christ's first coming and are before God's throne and before the Lamb wearing white robes and carrying palms in their hands. Israel must go through it because Israel did not know the Lord and will not know Him till He comes for His saints. Like Noah, Israel will have to go through the deluge; but, like Enoch, the saints of God will be caught up beforehand to meet Him in the air.

Another passage should be interpreted in the light of this truth: "*The Lord knoweth how to deliver the godly out of temptations, and to reserve the unjust unto the day of judgment to be punished*" (2 Peter 2:9). The godly will be taken out of the tribulation, but the unjust will be reserved to go through it.

In Luke 21, the words of the Lord Jesus suggest that we may hope to escape from this time of trouble: "*And when these things begin to come to pass, then look up, and lift up your heads; for your redemption draweth nigh*" (Luke 21:28). What "*things*" did He refer to? Distress of nations with perplexity, and tribulation terrors. Dr. Young translates this phrase *"Bend yourselves back, and lift up your heads..."* (YLT). Get ready for ascension; take the attitude of translation (see, for example, Hebrews 11:5); you are going up before the storm comes down. *"Bend yourselves back, and lift up your heads, because your redemption doth draw nigh"* (YLT). And then, the Lord added,

> Take heed to yourselves, lest at any time your hearts be overcharged with surfeiting, and drunkenness, and cares of this life, and so that day come upon you unawares. For as a snare shall it come on all them that dwell on the face of the whole earth. Watch ye therefore, and pray always, that ye may be accounted worthy to escape all these things that shall come to pass, and to stand before the Son of man.   (Luke 21:34–36)

Your place is up there with the Lord in the clouds, not down here in this earthly hell. Pray for that. Watch for that. Live for that—*"that ye may...escape all these things that shall come to pass, and...stand before the Son of man."*

Take No Chances

How should we therefore prepare to escape? We take no chances. Remember the five foolish virgins. (See Matthew 25:1–13.) They were virgins, and they were looking for the bridegroom, but they did not enter in to the wedding celebration. What became of them? Were they lost? Impossible. But they had to stay in the outer darkness of the tribulation night. They did not go in to the marriage of the Lamb. Doubtless, later, they had their place, but it was a second place. Thus, the Lord Jesus said, *"Be ye also ready: for in such an hour as ye think not the Son of man cometh"* (Matthew 24:44).

Someone asked Dr. A. J. Gordon if all believers would go up with the Lord when He came, or if only those who were walking with Him in holiness and separation would. They quoted that passage in Revelation about *"the firstfruits unto God and to the Lamb"* (Revelation 14:4), the holy ones *"which follow the Lamb whithersoever he goeth...and in their mouth was found no guile"* (Revelation 14:4–5). He was asked if only those would be caught up when Jesus Christ came, and the others would wait, or if all the people of God would be resurrected or translated. Dr. Gordon shook his head with a solemn, modest expression, and said, "I have not light enough to answer, but I would rather take no chances."

> I see that last red bloody sunset,
> I see the dread Avenger's form,
> I see the Armageddon onset,
> But I shall be above the storm.

> There comes a moaning and a sighing,
> There comes the tear-drop's heavy fall,
> The thousand agonies of dying,
> But I shall be beyond them all.[13]

CHAPTER NINE

THE PAROUSIA

"Behold, I come as a thief. Blessed is he that watcheth,
and keepeth his garments, lest he walk naked,
and they see his shame."
—Revelation 16:15

The two principal Greek words used to describe the second coming of the Lord Jesus are *parousia* and *epiphania*. The first literally means "presence," and the second means "appearing," or "manifestation." They have come to be recognized as describing the two aspects of the Lord's return—the first at the beginning of the tribulation; the second at its close and at the commencement of His millennial reign. The *parousia* will be for His saints, and it is this aspect of His coming that we will consider at this time.

Our text, Revelation 16:15, represents this coming as secret: *"Behold, I come as a thief."* When a thief comes to rob a home, he does not plan to steal the house and everything in it. He intends only to take away the treasures from it. Likewise, the Lord's coming will not bring about the dissolution of this world or the removal of its inhabitants; it will result in only the withdrawal of the little flock that will be found waiting for its Bridegroom. Furthermore, a thief does not send out a public announcement of his coming, nor allow the neighborhood to know about it; the first public evidence of his visit is seen after he has gone. In the same way, the world will not know that the Lord has come until it wakes some morning to find that all the best people have disappeared. It is of this that the Master says, *"One shall be taken, and the other left"* (Matthew 24:40).

Let us look at several important transactions that will be connected with the *parousia* of the Son of Man.

1. The First Resurrection

The principle of the resurrection is engraved upon the whole system of nature. The bulb of spring, the dying and germinating seed, and the evolution of the chrysalis and the butterfly all tell of life out of death. Chemistry continually illustrates the dissolution and reorganization of matter. In the presence of his audience, scientist and Christian lecturer Michael Faraday drops a little silver vase into a basin. Immediately, it is dissolved by the acid in the bowl, and he pours out the fluid to show that every fragment of the silver has disappeared. Then, he drops into that bowl another chemical; in a moment, the silver crystallizes at the bottom and is put in a crucible, melted, and poured into a mold. In a few minutes, Faraday holds up before his audience the silver vase reconstructed and shining in brilliant whiteness. It has passed through the laboratory of science and the process of resurrection. Well might Faraday ask, *"Why should it be thought a thing incredible with you, that God should raise the dead?"* (Acts 26:8).

Paul's Testimony

In 1 Corinthians 15, the apostle Paul gave us his sublime argument for the resurrection. First, he told us that we will receive a spiritual body. While it will be essentially the same as the mortal form that was laid in the dust, it will be incomparably more glorious. It will bear the same relation to our present body that the harvest field bears to the seed corn planted in it; or that the orange tree, all glorious with fruit and flowers, bears to the orange seed from which it sprang. To quote from another passage from Paul, the one is *"the body of our humiliation,"* the other *"the body of his glory"* (Philippians 3:21 YLT).

Again, the apostle told us that there is a fixed order in the resurrection. *"But every man in his own order"* (1 Corinthians 15:23)—literally, his own rank. This refers to the question of precedence at a social procession. In this grandest of all processions, every person will have his own proper rank: *"Christ the firstfruits; afterward they that are Christ's at his coming. Then cometh the end…"* (1 Corinthians 15:23–24). In the front rank of the resurrection, Christ Himself walks alone. In the second rank, those who are Christ's at His coming follow. In the third company, like a band of captives bringing up the rear, *"the dead, small and great, stand before God"* (Revelation 20:12). This latter company will not arise until after a thousand years of Christ's millennial reign.

Speaking of this first resurrection, the Lord Jesus used the expression, *"They which shall be accounted worthy to obtain that world, and the resurrection from the dead"* (Luke 20:35). In the third chapter of Philippians, the apostle Paul spoke of his great ambition: *"If by any means I might attain unto the resurrection of the dead"* (Philippians 3:11). In the familiar passage in his first epistle to the Thessalonians, the apostle again told us, *"The Lord himself shall descend from heaven with a shout,…and the dead in Christ shall rise first"* (1 Thessalonians 4:16). There is no reference to the wicked here, and there is no note of terror and judgment in all this comforting scene. It is a family gathering of the followers of the Lamb.

Revelation 20

But the most explicit passage relating to the resurrection is found in Revelation 20:

> *And I saw thrones, and they sat upon them, and judgment was given unto them: and I saw the souls of them that were beheaded for the witness ["testimony" YLT] of Jesus, and for the word of God, and which had not worshipped the beast, neither his image, neither had received his mark upon their foreheads, or in their hands; and they lived and reigned with Christ a thousand years. But the rest of the dead lived not again until the thousand years were finished. This is the first resurrection. Blessed and holy is he that hath part in the first resurrection: on such the second death hath no power, but they shall be priests of God and of Christ, and shall reign with him a thousand years.*   (Revelation 20:4–6)

There has been much discussion about this passage, and many attempts have been made to set aside its simple and literal force. We cannot find clearer or stronger language by which to express its force and vindicate its application to the resurrection of the saints at the coming of Christ than the following quotation from Dean Alford:

> I cannot consent to distort words from their plain sense and chronological place in the prophecy on account of any considerations of difficulty or any risk of abuses in connection with the doctrine of the Millennium. Those who lived nearest the apostles, and the whole Church for three hundred years, understood them in the plain, literal sense; and it is a strange sight in these days to see expositors who are among the first in reverence of antiquity casting aside the most cogent instance of consensus which the history of antiquity presents. As regards the text itself, no legitimate

treatment of it will extort what is known as the spiritual interpretation now in fashion. If, in a passage where two resurrections are mentioned, where certain of the dead lived again at the first, and the rest of the dead lived again only at the end of a specified period after the first—if in such a passage the first resurrection may be understood to mean spiritual rising with Christ, while the second means literal rising from the grave, then there is an end of all significance in language, and Scripture is wiped out as a definite testimony to anything. If the first resurrection is spiritual, then so is the second—which I suppose, none will be hardy enough to maintain—but if the second is literal, then so is the first, which, in common with the whole primitive Church and many of the best modern expositors, I do maintain and receive as an article of faith and hope.

The prophet Daniel appeared to refer to these two resurrections in Daniel 12:2, where he said, as translated by Samuel Tragelles, "Many of them that sleep in the dust of the earth shall awake; these (who awake) to everlasting life, and those (who do not awake) to shame and everlasting contempt."

The resurrection of the wicked dead comes at the close of Christ's millennial reign. Then will come what the Lord Jesus called *"the resurrection of condemnation"* (John 5:29 NKJV), when all the dead will stand before God. John told us further, *"And the sea gave up the dead which were in it; and death and hell delivered up the dead which were in them: and they were judged every man according to their works"* (Revelation 20:13).

2. The Translation of the Saints

Immediately after the resurrection of the dead in Christ will follow what is known as the rapture of the saints. The apostle Paul described it in 1 Thessalonians 4:

We which are alive and remain unto the coming of the Lord shall not prevent [precede] them which are asleep. For the Lord himself shall descend from heaven with a shout, with the voice of the archangel, and with the trump of God: and the dead in Christ shall rise first: then we which are alive and remain shall be caught up together with them in the clouds ["in clouds" YLT], to meet the Lord in the air: and so shall we ever be with the Lord. (1 Thessalonians 4:15–17)

How comforting it is to know that parted friends who separated at the graveside ages before will meet at His coming, and then will go on together in loving recognition and glorious fellowship in the chariots of ascension, with ample time to renew the broken intimacies of the past as they ascend the skies, until, at length, the Master's presence will burst upon their vision, and they will *"ever be with the Lord."*

Enoch and Elijah represent these translated ones. "Born out of due time" (see 1 Corinthians 15:8) as types of their future followers, they lead the glorious procession. A great multitude that no person can number (see Revelation 7:9) will be waiting for that whispered summons that will reach every longitude of the earth's surface at the same blissful moment. In one place, it will be midnight, and two will be sleeping together. *"The one shall be taken, and the other shall be left"* (Luke 17:34). In another place farther east, it will be dawn, and two women in some village will be *"grinding at the mill"* (Matthew 24:41) and preparing their morning breakfast; and again, *"the one shall be taken, and the other left"* (Matthew 24:41). Still farther east, perhaps on the wheat fields of Russia or the rice fields of Japan, *"two men will be in the field"* (Matthew 24:40 NKJV). Suddenly, the one will disappear, and upon the other will burst the fearful truth, "The Lord has come, and I am left behind."

3. The Marriage of the Lamb

The *parousia* of Christ will be followed by some beatific joy that the Lord Himself described as the marriage of the King's Son. (See Matthew 22:20.) Throughout the Bible, the marriage bond runs like a golden thread, linking the scenes of the first paradise with the glories of paradise restored. While the figure has not always been worthy of its highest meaning because of the imperfection of human love, yet, as little bits of broken glass can each reflect a whole sun, so our poor, imperfect earthly unions have in them the promise and prophecy of heaven.

The Bride of Christ

We trace this golden thread through the story of Rebekah's wooing (see Genesis 24), the Forty-fifth Psalm, and the book of Song of Solomon, as well as Paul's fine image of the church as the bride of Christ (see Ephesians 5:22–32). But in the book of Revelation, this figure is clothed with still higher majesty and glory. There we see the bride *"arrayed in fine linen, clean and white"* (Revelation 19:8), and we see the heavenly procession as it follows the glorious Leader (see Revelation 19:14). There we see the home to which He brings her in the New Jerusalem. And there we see her beauty transcending all the gems of earth. (See Revelation 21:1–3, 9–12, 18–24.)

Two Classes

The parable of the ten virgins in Matthew 25 gives us a far-off vision of the marriage supper of the Lamb and suggests with solemn warning the danger that some may miss their place in that blessed company. Surely, there must be a difference between the saintly souls who have been tried and have been "washed and made white" (see Revelation 7:14) and the men and women who have found their happiness in the things of the world and would not understand the rapture of the Bridegroom's love. Are these earth-stained souls, even if saved at last, to have the same place as John of Patmos and Bernard of Cluny; of Mary of Bethany and Monica of Hippo? Surely, the question is enough to make us pause and ask our hearts if it is worthwhile to run the risk.

What would an earthly marriage be without love? Then what will heaven mean if we do not already know the betrothal of the heart to our heavenly Bridegroom and the rapture of His love?

Have we seen Him in His beauty? Have we hearkened to His call? Have we been won by His love? Accordingly, let us learn this:

> For O the Master is so fair,
> His smile so sweet to banished men,
> That they who meet Him anywhere,
> Can never rest on earth again.
>
> And they who see Him risen afar,
> At God's right hand for sinful men,
> Forgetful stand, of home and land,
> Remembering fair Jerusalem.

CHAPTER TEN

THE JUDGMENT OF THE SAINTS

Three judgments are distinguished in the New Testament:

1. The judgment of the saints at the Lord's coming
2. The judgment of the nations at the commencement of the millennium
3. The judgment of the wicked at the close of the millennium

We will now consider the first of these judgments.

Not a Judgment of Condemnation

The judgment of the saints will not be a judgment of condemnation. Those who are to take part in it have already been justified. The Scriptures say:

> *Who shall lay any thing to the charge of God's elect? It is God that justifieth. Who is he that condemneth? It is Christ that died, yea rather, that is risen again, who is even at the right hand of God....* (Romans 8:33–34)

He that heareth my word, and believeth on him that sent me,
hath everlasting life, and shall not come into condemnation
["judgment" YLT, NKJV]; *but is passed from death unto life.*

(John 5:24)

This will not be a judgment to decide the future destiny of the saints. That is decided by their sonship and saintship. The moment the believer passes from the earth, he is with his Lord in rest and glory.

A Judgment of Inspection and Reward

The judgment of the saints will be a judgment only of reward and inspection. It will be a vindication of them before all people against all charges and misunderstandings.

Therefore judge nothing before the time, until the Lord come,
who both will bring to light the hidden things of darkness, and
will make manifest the counsels of the hearts: and then shall
every man have praise of God.   (1 Corinthians 4:5)

This is very gracious. God will come to search out and bring to light the secret motives, the love that the world knew nothing of; and, forgetting and hiding His children's faults, He will see and show only what He can praise.

It will be a judgment of inspection. Only that which was put there by the Holy Spirit will stand—that which was the spirit and life of Jesus. All else will be dropped out; that alone will remain. The wood, hay, and stubble will burn up in the testing fire, and the gold and silver and precious stones of God's own faith and love and holiness will be left with more intense brightness. (See 1 Corinthians 3:10–15.)

It will also bring to each one his and her just reward for service, according to the principles of righteousness and the measure and quality of service.

The judgment of the saints will determine the future place and service of the saints in the millennial kingdom. They are to be the rulers of the future age, and each one's position will be determined by his special character and adaptation.

In the great empire of China, every government post is filled not by political preferment but as the result of competitive examinations. Education, therefore, can raise the poorest and humblest man to the highest office in the land. According to the standing of the students at the close of their annual competitive examinations, they are promoted to all grades, from mayor to mandarin.[14] So, in the far higher application of this principle, the thrones and principalities of the Millennial Age will be filled as the result of this inspection, and Christ will return to this earth with all His officers of state selected from the experience of a lifetime already spent amid the discipline of earth.

Principles Regarding the Judgment

The following are the principles upon which the judgment of the saints will be based and made plain.

It Will Be Based on Reward

First, there is a distinction between salvation and reward. Salvation is altogether free; reward is bestowed for service rendered. In a college course, there are subjects that all students must take, as well as honor classes that are entered only by those who especially compete for prizes. Similarly, in the kingdom of God, all must repent, believe, and be born again; but all may not be heroes of faith or service or sacrifice, and all will not wear garlands and crowns of glory. The workers in the parable of the laborers in the vineyard may represent the principle of the common salvation (see Matthew 20:1–16), while the parable of the talents (see Matthew 25:14–30) and the parable of the pounds (see Luke 19:13–27) may represent the principle of rewards at the Lord's coming.

These words of Christ to the woman of Samaria, *"If thou knewest the gift of God"* (John 4:10), describe salvation; His words just afterward to the disciples refer to the reward: *"He that reapeth* **receiveth wages***, and* **gathereth fruit** *unto life eternal: that both he that soweth and he that reapeth may rejoice together"* (John 4:36). This is addressed to the disciples (the servants), and it describes the double reward for service: wages—paid as they do the work— and a share in the fruit at harvesttime.

Let us look at a striking passage from 1 Corinthians:

> *Know ye not that they which run in a race run all, but one receiveth the prize?…I therefore so run, not as uncertainly; so fight I, not as one that beateth the air: but I keep under my body, and bring it into subjection: lest that by any means, when I have preached to others, I myself should be a castaway.*
>
> (1 Corinthians 9:24, 26–27)

The word *"castaway"* would more correctly be translated "a disapproved competitor." It literally means one rejected at the end of the race as regards the prize—not finally lost, for such a thought never entered Paul's mind.

It Will Be According to Works

Second, the reward is according to service rendered. It is in exact proportion—not always to the quantity but to the spirit and value. How finely this is brought out in the parable of the pounds. Five pounds multiplied brings five cities, and ten pounds improved brings ten cities. The doubling of one talent is as much rewarded as the doubling of five. The humblest worker, if fully faithful, is recompensed as fully as the most illustrious. *"He that receiveth a prophet in the name of a prophet shall receive a prophet's reward; and he that receiveth a righteous man in the name of a righteous man shall receive a righteous man's reward"* (Matthew 10:41). The service that was in the heart to do, but for which we had no opportunity, will be rewarded. *"For if there be first a willing mind, it is accepted according to that a man hath, and not according to that he hath not"* (2 Corinthians 8:12 NKJV). Many a quiet heart will be brought out into the light of heaven as the true instrument of a blessing in which others, perhaps, had a more public part.

Some of the special recompenses are definitely described. There are wages and fruit for the reaper in life's harvest (see John 4:36), and glories like the eternal stars for those who *"turn many to righteousness"* (Daniel 12:3). There is *"a crown of glory that fadeth not away"* for the faithful minister. (See 1 Peter 5:1–4.) There is a *"crown of life"* for the one who bravely and truly stands in the battlefield of life and endures the ordeal of temptation. (See James 1:12.) These bitter strokes are fashioning our diadem for the by-and-by. Then the suffering martyr will find his blood drops crystallized into the rubies of a *"crown of life."* (See Revelation 2:10.) Then those who simply overcome will receive a royal heritage with Christ Himself. (See, for example, Revelation 3:21.) And even those who could do little else than live and look for His appearing will be recompensed with *"a crown of righteousness."* (See 2 Timothy 4:8.)

The one who has faithfully used his natural talents will receive in proportion to his improvement of them, and he who has multiplied and rightly employed his spiritual privileges and endowments will be made a ruler over as many cities as the "pounds" he accrued. The faithful and wise steward who took good care of his Lord's household here and gave to his children a portion in season will be made *"ruler over all that he hath"* (Luke 12:44). And those who left all and followed Christ will be recompensed a hundred-fold more in that time in the things they sacrificed for Christ. (See Matthew 19:27–29.) Even the secret thought of service that was never expressed will be recognized and recompense, and *"every man have praise of God*" (1 Corinthians 4:5). Neither will our gifts to His treasury be lost. The generous millionaire and the self-denying widow will find all their gifts on deposit, at compound interest, and they will stand astonished at their colossal fortunes. Like the crowns of the time of the Jewish restoration after the exile, which were forged out of the golden gifts of the captives of Babylon (see Zechariah 6:9–11), their gold will be found hanging in diadems above their heads on heaven's pillars, inscribed with their names inwrought with His. Oh, then, no sacrifice will seem to have been too great, no gift too large, no love too warm, no enthusiasm too intense. Life's full significance will be unrolled, and our only regret will be that we cannot live it over again.

CHAPTER ELEVEN

THE EPIPHANY AND THE MILLENNIAL REIGN

*"And I saw thrones, and they sat upon them, and judgment
was given unto them…: and they lived and reigned with
Christ a thousand years."*
—Revelation 20:4

The coming of the Lord with His saints will follow the tribulation and usher in the millennium. This was the earliest prophecy of the advent: *"And Enoch also, the seventh from Adam, prophesied of these, saying, Behold, the Lord cometh with ten thousands of his saints, to execute judgment upon all…"* (Jude 14–15). This is the obvious order of the twentieth chapter of Revelation, where the thousand years follow the destruction of Antichrist, the binding of Satan, and the first resurrection.

A Public Epiphany

The epiphany of the Lord Jesus, unlike His *parousia*, will be public and visible to all the world. This is what John saw when he cried, "*Behold, he cometh with clouds; and every eye shall see him*" (Revelation 1:7). This is what the Master meant when He testified, "*Then shall appear the sign of the Son of man in heaven: and then shall all the tribes of the earth mourn, and they shall see the Son of man coming in the clouds of heaven with power and great glory*" (Matthew 24:30; see also Revelation 1:7); and again, "*When the Son of man shall come in his glory,…then shall he sit upon the throne of his glory: and before him shall be gathered all nations*" (Matthew 25:31–32).

Poets have seen the golden age afar, as the mirage is seen upon the desert sky. Ancient seers have painted its glowing outlines in words and images they could not themselves understand; and living and dying patriarchs and saints have looked forward to it with great desire, as to "*a city which hath foundations, whose builder and maker is God*" (Hebrews 11:10) and to "*a better country, that is, an heavenly*" (Hebrews 11:16).

Man has tried to make his own millennium. Poetry has dreamed of it and degraded it into a sensuous paradise. Patriots and optimists have drawn the vision of a golden age of liberty, equality, peace, and plenty, and have seen only anarchy, license, and misery arise at the touch of their deceptive wand. Moralists have toiled for purity, temperance, and virtue, and dreamed of a day when social reform will have blotted out the last spot of plague from our cities—only to see wickedness, crime, and the curse of alcohol and woman's shame increase with increasing civilization. And Christian reformers have expected a spiritual millennium in which the gospel will cover the myriad populations of earth and make every land a holy, happy paradise of love and purity. But alas! The lands that are most evangelized are sometimes the farthest from millennial piety or purity. And if, tomorrow, all the world was to reach the condition to which Christian lands have attained in the three centuries since the Reformation, earth would still be a sight to break the heart of Him who died for us.

No, God has something better for His weary, hungry children than any of man's counterfeit millenniums.

> There is a fount about to stream;
> There is an age about to beam;
> There is a midnight darkness turning into grey;
> Men of faith and men of action, clear the way.

Features and Events of the Millennial Age

Let us look at some of the features and events of the Millennial Age, which will follow the Lord's glorious appearing.

A World Without Satan

The first feature of the picture is a world without the devil—without his instigations, temptations, deceptions, and destructive activities. At the very beginning, he will be bound by a strong angel and shut up in the bottomless pit for a thousand years, so that he may deceive the nations no more, until the thousand years are finished. (See Revelation 3:20.) No doubt, Satan has gotten credit for much evil that humanity alone is to blame for. But, after all allowances are made, the vast aggregate of human sin and misery is due to Satan's terrific power and the influence of the countless myrmidons of his kingdom who will be cast out with him. Think of his awful delusions; his desperate possession of oppressed spirits; his wild and fearful ravages over the minds of the insane; his monstrous crimes, lusts, cruelties, and deceptions; and then realize that all this will be absent from that happy age, and you will begin to comprehend what a tangible reality the millennium is to be.

An Age Without Evil Systems

Not only will Satan be cast out, but also the great systems of evil through which he has governed men. These include, first, the forms of human government that have oppressed the world since the days of Egypt; second, the forms of false religion that have worshipped Satan in the name of God and sanctioned every enormity and evil under the guise of good. Of these religions, three especially have been the curse of the ages, namely, Romanism, Islam, and paganism. These will be cast out. The first two will be hurled into the abyss with Satan; the last will be subdued by the diffusion of the gospel in the Millennial Age. What an incalculable sum of misery and sin has come into the world through false governments and false religions. What a brood of vices and curses has sprung from the corrupt Papacy and the vile Muslim faith. But these fountains will no longer defile the world. The worship of saints and martyrs, the mysteries of the confessional and the conventual life, the sealed Bible and the superstitious ritual of ten thousand altars will no longer insult heaven or deceive humankind. The sensual excesses, the despotic tyranny, the desolating cruelty, and the deadly nightshade of Islam will be lifted from earth's fairest regions, and the early home of the human family will become a second Eden. And over all the vaster fields of heathendom, there will no longer ascend the smoke of cruel and unholy sacrifices, or be heard the cries of suffering and wrong, and the death-gasp of despair.

The Abolishment of Wickedness and War

Not only will Satan and his chosen instruments be abolished, but the wickedness of the wicked will also come to an end, and the earth will be filled with righteousness and peace.

> *In his days shall the righteous flourish; and abundance of peace so long as the moon endureth.*   (Psalm 72:7)

> *They shall not hurt nor destroy in all my holy mountain: for the earth shall be full of the knowledge of the LORD, as the waters cover the sea.*   (Isaiah 11:9)

Nation shall not lift up a sword against nation, neither shall they learn war any more.   (Micah 4:3)

And many nations shall come, and say, Come, and let us go up to the mountain of the LORD, and to the house of the God of Jacob; and he will teach us of his ways, and we will walk in his paths: for the law shall go forth of Zion, and the word of the LORD from Jerusalem.   (Micah 4:2)

We do not say that there will be no sin left in human hearts during the Millennial Age but that open wickedness will be suppressed and restrained under the holy and universal sway of Christ and His saints. The world will be evangelized and brought into subjugation to Christ; and, ostensibly, at least, it will be righteous and obedient. Thrice-happy day of peace and righteousness, hasten your appearing and bring the vision of waiting ages to this brokenhearted world.

> Down the dark future, through long generations,
> The echoing sounds grow fainter and then cease;
> And like a bell, with solemn, sweet vibrations,
> I hear once more the voice of Christ say, "Peace!"
>
> Peace! and no longer from its brazen portals
> The blast of War's great organ shakes the skies!
> But beautiful as songs of the immortals,
> The holy melodies of love arise.[15]

The Visible Presence of the Lord Jesus

It will, above all other glories, enjoy the personal, visible, and continual presence of Christ Himself, its glorious King.

The LORD shall be king over all the earth. (Zechariah 14:9)

There shall come forth a rod out of the stem of Jesse, and a Branch shall grow out of his roots: and the Spirit of the LORD shall rest upon him, the spirit of wisdom and understanding, the spirit of counsel and might, the spirit of knowledge and of the fear of the LORD;...with righteousness shall he judge the poor, and reprove with equity for the meek of the earth....And righteousness shall be the girdle of his loins, and faithfulness the girdle of his reins.   (Isaiah 11:1–2, 4–5)

Sing and rejoice, O daughter of Zion: for, lo, I come, and I will dwell in the midst of thee, saith the LORD.   (Zechariah 2:10)

Son of man, the place of my throne, and the place of the soles of my feet, where I will dwell in the midst of the children of Israel for ever....   (Ezekiel 43:7)

And the name of the city from that day shall be, The LORD is there.   (Ezekiel 48:35)

The kingdoms of this world are become the kingdoms of our Lord, and of his Christ.   (Revelation 11:15)

These two facts alone are enough to make a heaven: the absence of Satan and the presence of the Lord Jesus. Earth will again be His residence. He will be its benignant and glorious King. He will, no doubt, be accessible and visible to His subjects, as was Solomon of old. Once a year, Zechariah tells us, the nations will come up to Jerusalem to worship Him and to see His blessed and glorious face. He will especially be the friend of the lowly and the poor.

He shall judge the poor of the people, he shall save the children of the needy, and shall break in pieces the oppressor....He shall come down like rain upon the mown grass: as showers that water the earth. In his days shall the righteous flourish;

and abundance of peace so long as the moon endureth....He
shall spare the poor and needy, and shall save the souls of the
needy.   (Psalm 72:4, 6–7, 13)

To His risen and translated saints, He will be especially near. "*They shall see his face; and his name shall be in their foreheads*" (Revelation 22:4). "*The Lamb which is in the midst of the throne shall feed them, and shall lead them unto living fountains of waters*" (Revelation 7:17). His majesty and glory will shed divine effulgence over all the earth. Brighter than the glory of the sunlight will be the splendor of His presence. "*The city had no need of the sun,...for the glory of God did lighten it, and the Lamb is the light thereof*" (Revelation 21:23). Then, Christ's dying prayer for us will be fulfilled:

Father, I will that they also, whom thou hast given me, be with
me where I am; that they may behold my glory, which thou
hast given me: for thou lovedst me before the foundation of the
world.   (John 17:24)

Some sweet morn we'll see His face,
And we shall be satisfied;
Some sweet day in His embrace
We shall evermore abide.[16]

Glorified with Him and Like Him

Not only will we have the presence of the Lord Jesus, but our own state will be as glorious as His. We will be like Him, and He will say of us, "*The glory which thou gavest me I have given them; that they may be one, even as we are one*" (John 17:22). We will bear the image of His resurrection body. We will have His marvelous beauty and His mighty powers. Clothed in immortal youth and divine energy, we will know no pain or weakness; we will feel our beings thrill with the pulses of His glorious life and the rapture and ecstasy of eternal health and strength. We will rise superior to distance and matter, traversing space with the celerity of an angel's wing, and perhaps controlling matter with the resistless hand of His own power, and permitted to share His own creative might and authority. But, more glorious still, our spiritual and intellectual nature will be conformed to His likeness. We will be holy as He is holy. (See 1 Peter 1:16.) We will reflect His very face and beauty. We will *"shine forth as the sun in the kingdom of* [our] *Father"* (Matthew 13:43). We will know, even as we also are known. (See 1 Corinthians 13:12.) We will see all things with His eyes. We will love as the flaming seraphim and rejoice with all the transports of heavenly blessedness.

> All that He has shall be mine,
> All that He is I shall be,
> Robed in His glory divine,
> I shall be even as He.

During the Millennial Age, the home of the glorified saints will be the New Jerusalem. As nearly as we can judge from the later description of the New Jerusalem after the millennium, it would seem to be a city in the skies, of exceeding glory, just above the earth and in constant communion with it.

In this higher region, the children of the resurrection will dwell with Christ, their Lord and King, and from that place will go forth to administer the government of the world below them. Their life will thus be different from the nations of the human family who will still succeed each other during all this age. There will thus be two races—the immortal ones who will reign with Christ in the heavenly city, and the children of mortality who will still remain in their successive generations upon the earth. The state of the former will be immeasurably superior. The latter may, perhaps, be translated one by one and exalted to it, like Enoch, as they faithfully finish their course from generation to generation.

Exalted Service

We will not only have a glorious place and character but also a most exalted service. We will reign with Christ on the earth. That is, we will administer, with Him and with His endowments of wisdom and power, the government of earth. To each of us, He will give two cities or ten, as we have been qualified by the discipline and service of our life. Some will be sent forth to take direction of the material improvement of earth's barren wastes; some to build the cities of those busy years; some to organize society among the masses of the converted nations; some to inspire and direct the spiritual activities of that age. David will once more reorganize the throne of Judah and rule with his greater Son over his ancient house, while, perhaps, Solomon, Jehoshaphat, Hezekiah, and Isaiah may be his illustrious court. Paul will no doubt muster the roll of the Gentile nations and rejoice at the completion and fruition of his apostolate. Luther may be a prince again where he was a prisoner. Livingstone may be permitted to lift up Africa at last and to see it rise from Table Mountain to Atlas snows into a paradise of beauty and blessing.

Honor and Work

But we bid speculation be hushed, and we rest in knowing that to each of us will be given the honor and the work for which our experience, our service, and our sacrifices here have prepared and entitled us. *"To sit on my right hand, and on my left,"* said Christ to His disciples James and John, *"is not mine to give, but it shall be given to them for whom it is prepared of My Father"* (Matthew 20:23). The Lord Jesus had also asked them, *"Are ye able to drink of the cup that I shall drink of, and to be baptized with the baptism that I am baptized with?"* (Matthew 20:22). And, elsewhere, He said to His disciples, *"Ye which have followed me, in the regeneration when the Son of man shall sit in the throne of his glory, ye also shall sit upon twelve thrones, judging the twelve tribes of Israel"* (Luke 22:30).

Reunited with Departed Friends

The millennium will also bring us our departed friends. We will see again the unforgotten faces and clasp the immortal hands. We will wonder at their beauty and glory, and will understand all the mystery of the parting. And, like the meeting of Joseph and his brothers, we will see with amazement how the goodness of God has made all things work together for good. (See Genesis 50:19–20; Romans 8:29.) All tears will be wiped away, and all hearts will swell with rapture to know that we can never weep or be parted again. (See Revelation 21:4.)

Earth Restored

But the millennium will also bring the restoration and evangelization of earth. Not all the glory of those years will center on the resplendent palaces of the New Jerusalem. But this terrestrial scene *"shall be glad for them; and the desert shall rejoice, and blossom as the rose"* (Isaiah 35:1). Two races will occupy the millennial earth. First, the Jewish nation, already previously restored to its own land, will be the Queen of Nations, and from Jerusalem it will once more reestablish its sway to the utmost confines of its ancient boundaries.

But the Gentile peoples will also be left on earth, in all their myriad populations, and will at the very earliest period of the millennial reign be converted to Christ and be raised to all the immunities, privileges, and blessings of the highest Christian civilization. In this great missionary movement, the Jews are to be largely instrumental; and, under the fostering government of Christ Himself—the King of kings—and the wisest men of all the past, they are to advance to a prosperity and happiness never imagined in the wildest utopian dreams of poets or statesmen.

Physically, the earth will no doubt be considerably altered, and its geographical and climatic conditions rendered more favorable and delightful. We know that a glorious river is going to spring from the rocks underneath the sanctuary and flow eastward and westward in fertilizing beauty to the Dead Sea and the Mediterranean Sea. (See Ezekiel 47:1–12.) Other lands may be similarly changed. The highest intellectual and spiritual culture, and the supernatural wisdom and power of God, will soon transform the most rugged deserts of earth into an Eden of beauty and joy. Socially and politically, all will be pure, just, and happy. Misgovernment and corruption will not enter there. The world will reach its highest development, and God will show what Eden might have been, except for sin—or, rather, how *"where sin abounded, grace did much more abound"* (Romans 5:20).

CHAPTER TWELVE

THE NEW HEAVENS AND NEW EARTH

"And I saw a new heaven and a new earth: for the first
heaven and the first earth were passed away."
—Revelation 21:1

A thousand years of millennial blessedness have quickly passed. The happy years have flown, and the earth has grown not older but younger, and has long ago robed herself with the beauty and gladness of paradise restored. The teeming nations have multiplied to billions, and the generations that have been born have not even had the memory of a time when life was not a blessing and a joy. Righteousness has seemed so blessed and so easy that sin has not had power to tempt, and virtue has perhaps grown to be a habit rather than a principle.

Is Human Nature Any Better?

Outwardly, the world has been conformed to the will and government of Christ; but it is to be feared that, inwardly, multitudes have not really been converted. It might easily be demonstrated that, if really tested, human nature is not inherently any better, and that if the favorable circumstances were withdrawn, the old wickedness might burst forth like a volcano with undiminished fury and malignity.

The Test Comes

It is not long before the opportunity is given. At the end of the thousand years, Satan is loosed out of his prison and permitted once more to visit the world. Perhaps this opportunity is designed to be a test even to the devil.

Satan Is Irredeemably Evil

Why should we wonder if God is willing to give even Satan a second chance to show if there is any improvement in him? After a thousand years in his gloomy penitentiary, he is permitted once more to leave his prison and to see for himself the grace and loveliness of Christ and the blessedness of His benignant reign. Over all the happy regions of earth, he beholds the fruits of righteousness and the blessings of religion, compared with the six thousand years of his own destructive rule. Does he appreciate the difference? Does he recognize the beauty and blessedness of obedience and submission to a good and righteous God? Does he decide to let these happy tribes alone in the peaceful enjoyment of their Creator's love? Does he manifest the least desire to amend his course and to share in the blessings of the scene that he beholds?

Not for a moment!

Satan Prompts a Great Revolt, as in Eden

Before Satan is banished forever to his dismal dungeon, it must be shown to the universe that he is utterly, irredeemably, and hopelessly wicked, and that, for the sake of the universe, he must be eternally destroyed, restrained from doing further harm. And so, for a moment longer, he is left to his own wicked will.

He is not slow to take advantage of it. Burning with fury at the happiness of his victims and the ruin of all his ages of work, he swoops upon his prey with all his ancient cunning. Aided, perhaps, by his countless myrmidons, he whispers into the hearts of people the wild thought of a great rebellion and a free and independent government unfettered by the "despotic" will of yonder King.

It is easy to paint the glories of a great republic. It is easy to magnify the hardships of obedience. It is easy for men who never saw the ages of sin to forget the fruits of disobedience. It is easy for proud human nature to pervert its prosperity and blessings and use them as instruments of aggrandizement and evil. How vast must seem their resources, how reasonable must seem their demand for independence, and how brilliant must seem the picture of the serpent's dream. It is the story of Eden again. Humanity falls once more. Like wildfire, the infatuation sweeps over the nations.

The Revolt

Perhaps himself incarnate, as a brilliant and magnetic leader—a Napoleon and Apollyon (see Revelation 9:11) of policy and genius—Satan gathers and holds people to him in the spell of his influence until a host, gathered from earth's remotest nations and as limitless as the sands of the sea, is marching behind his banner and even surrounding the very seat of divine government and the walls of the Holy City. (See Revelation 20:7–9.)

The races that will chiefly follow him are strangely growing into prominence today as, concurrently, the revolutionary and the imperial elements of our age. Russia is the expression of despotic tyranny, and that nation is also the hotbed of anarchy, lawlessness, and revolution. It is from this people that the final Gog and Magog are to come. (See Revelation 20:8.) Ezekiel describes a terrible invasion of the same warlike races, but it seems to be at an earlier stage and probably precedes the millennium. (See Ezekiel 38:14–39:29.)

Fire from Heaven

The conflict is not long. Not now, as in former ages, is Satan to gain a foothold and prolong the conflict of good and evil. One little hour is given to show his worst and to let the world see what sinners can be even after a thousand years of love. And then, by one fiery wave, he and his followers are swept from the scene forever, and he is buried under chains and flames beyond the possibility of release or return. (See Revelation 20:9–10.)

The Final Catastrophe

And then there bursts upon the universe the great, the dread, the final catastrophe. The last act of sin is over; its awful course finished. The universe must be purged of its longest and latest stain. All that it has touched must be purified in God's cleansing fire, and a new universe must emerge without a shadow of the evil past.

The Dead Are Raised

First comes the resurrection of the dead of all past ages. "*I saw the dead, small and great, stand before God....And the sea gave up the dead which were in it; and death and hell delivered up the dead which were in them*" (Revelation 20:12–13). The myriad dead who had fallen through the ages and slumbered on through the first resurrection and the Millennial Age are rudely awakened to behold a world in flames and the majestic terrors of the great white throne. Not one of them will be lost sight of. Bearing the traces of their sinful lives and the marks of their inward character, they will stand before the Judge. It will be a sight of unutterable sorrow. The vision of it looming from afar has brought the tears to Mercy's weeping eyes and led her to reach out her hands to reckless people in imploring love, crying, *"Flee from the wrath to come"* (Matthew 3:7; Luke 3:7).

The Judgment

They have come for judgment. Mercy is not there. Long before this, she has folded her brood beneath her tender wing, and she stands afar off, turning her face away from this sad and dreadful sight. The righteous are not there. Their judgment is long since past. They have no place there, except perhaps as judges by the side of the great Arbiter of destiny. Beloved, keep out of this judgment. Keep out of this place. It is too late for mercy there. *"He who hears My word and believes in Him who sent Me has everlasting life, and shall not come into judgment, but has passed from death into life"* (John 5:24 NKJV).

It is a judgment according to works. There are several books. (See Revelation 20:12.) There is the book of evidence, or facts. Perhaps nature has folded away, like the wax pages of the phonograph, all the scenes and sounds of the past, and will unroll them in that day before the eyes of all people. Perhaps memory is a volume of finest tissue pages whose filmy leaves will someday open and, in the fiery breath of that hour, become vivid and plain. No one will dispute the records, and no one will answer back. Time will be given for every excuse, every ameliorating circumstance, every question and reason. There will be no hurry, and there will be no capricious fury. A patient, long-suffering, and righteous God, who knows full well how hard the easiest sentence is, will not be swift to destroy the last hope of those poor, helpless souls.

But there will be strict justice and fidelity to the statute book of the universe. This will be the second book, God's Word. And there will also be the book of conscience. Those who had no Bible will be judged by the inner law, *"(...the law written in their hearts, their conscience also bearing witness, and their thoughts the mean while accusing or else excusing one another;) in the day when God shall judge the secrets of men…"* (Romans 2:15–16).

There will be yet another book, the Book of Life. This is the record of the redeemed. Having one's name recorded there answers all other charges. Through the blood of the Lord Jesus Christ, all claims are settled, and we have life everlasting. And all whose names are not found written in the Book of Life are cast into the lake of fire. (See Revelation 20:15.)

The New Heavens and New Earth

Then will come a mighty conflagration. A cyclone of flame will sweep over the universe and change its character and appearance as completely, perhaps, as when, from the chaotic wreck of the first creation, the present earth emerged.

And when the fire has done its work, the new creation will come forth in Edenic and eternal loveliness and purity, never to be sullied again, never to echo a sigh of pain or a cry of hate, never to be stained with human blood again, never to bear thorns and nourish serpents again, but to be the eternal home of peace and purity and love, and the scene where, through *"the ages to come* [God] *might show the exceeding riches of his grace in his kindness toward us through Christ Jesus"* (Ephesians 2:7).

The New Jerusalem

And I saw a new heaven and a new earth: for the first heaven and the first earth were passed away; and there was no more sea. And I John saw the holy city, new Jerusalem, coming down from God out of heaven, prepared as a bride adorned for her husband. And I heard a great voice out of heaven saying, Behold, the tabernacle of God is with men, and he will dwell with them, and they shall be his people, and God himself shall be with them, and be their God. And God shall wipe away all tears from their eyes; and there shall be no more death, neither sorrow, nor crying, neither shall there be any more pain: for the former things are passed away. And he that sat upon the throne said, Behold, I make all things new. And he said unto me, Write: for these words are true and faithful. And he said unto me, It is done. I am Alpha and Omega, the beginning and the end. I will give unto him that is athirst of the fountain of the water of life freely. He that overcometh shall inherit all things; and I will be his God, and he shall be my son. But the fearful, and unbelieving, and the abominable, and murderers, and whoremongers, and sorcerers, and idolaters, and all liars, shall have their part in the lake which burneth with fire and brimstone: which is the second death....And the twelve gates were twelve pearls: every several gate was of one pearl: and the street of the city was pure gold, as it were transparent glass. And I saw no temple therein: for the Lord God Almighty and the Lamb are the temple of it. And the city had no need of the sun, neither of the moon, to shine in it: for the glory of God did lighten it, and the Lamb is the light thereof. And the nations of them which are saved shall walk in the light of it: and the kings of the earth do bring their glory and honour into it. And the gates of it shall not be shut at all by day: for there shalt be no night there. And they shall bring the glory and honour of the nations into it. And there shall in no wise enter into it any thing that defileth, neither whatsoever worketh abomination, or maketh a lie: but they which are written in the Lamb's book of life. (Revelation 21:1–8, 21–27)

The River of Water of Life and the Tree of Life

And he showed me a pure river of water of life, clear as crystal, proceeding out of the throne of God and of the Lamb. In the midst of the street of it, and on either side of the river, was there the tree of life, which bare twelve manner of fruits, and yielded her fruit every month: and the leaves of the tree were for the healing of the nations. And there shall be no more curse: but the throne of God and of the Lamb shall be in it; and his servants shall serve him: and they shall see his face; and his name shall be in their foreheads. And there shall be no night there; and they need no candle, neither light of the sun; for the Lord God giveth them light: and they shall reign for ever and ever. (Revelation 22:1–5)

A Reconstructed Universe

There will be new heavens, and there will be a new earth, and the characteristic of both will be *"wherein dwelleth righteousness"* (2 Peter 3:13). Perhaps even the very heavens, too, have been made unclean and need the touch of fire. There are traces of great convulsions in yonder worlds. Has there been sin there, too? We cannot tell. But there will be sin no more in the ages to come. Earth and heaven will be more closely linked, perhaps, than now. The earth will still be the habitation of the human race. Successive generations will still people it, and the nations of the saved will still multiply upon it. How else can God fulfill His promises to His ancient people, so often given and declared to last through "a thousand generations"? How else could we read in Revelation 21 of the New Jerusalem that, after the new heavens and the new earth will have come, *"the nations of them which are saved shall walk in the light of it: and the kings of the earth do bring their glory and honour into it"* (Revelation 21:24)?

Perhaps this earth will be too small for all these multiplied races. Perhaps that is the reason why the new heavens are to be prepared. Maybe they will be the colonies of the earth and the redeemed confederacies of the skies. Maybe the true and tried servants of the Lord will be made the princes and the rulers of yonder stars of light, with a whole world of beings to love and bless. And perhaps we will pass from one to another on wings of swiftness and power, traversing the universe of God as illimitably as our thoughts can sweep over it now, and knowing all the heights and depths of the unfathomable wisdom, power, and love of Him who makes us partakers of His nature and His throne.

Our Eternal Home

The New Jerusalem will be the home of the glorified saints and the seat of the throne of God and the Lamb. Earth will become the "metropolis of immensity." *"The tabernacle of God is with men, and he will dwell with them, and they shall be his people, and God himself shall be with them, and be their God"* (Revelation 21:3). It will not be a literal city on the earth but a suspended city in the clouds. John saw it descending from God out of heaven, as bright and beautiful as a mountain of pearls and precious stones, flashing with all the colors of the rainbow and shining with the glory of God Himself, more marvelous than all His works. (See Revelation 21:10–12, 18–21.)

Its dimensions are given, showing clearly that it is a separate, material substance above, not on the earth. It is a solid cube, its length, breadth, and height equal. Its streets will not run only hither and thither, but also up and down. There will be no law of gravitation there, for it itself will be the center of all power and motion. Its immense dimensions will be *376 miles each way.* (See Revelation 21:15–17.) A grand and glorious city, indeed! Royal mother and majestic home of all the great and good of earth and heaven! Need we wonder that, as its glories have sometimes broken through the mists of time, the homesick hearts of God's dear saints have sighed and sung like the following?

For thee, O dear, dear country! mine eyes their vigils keep,
For very love beholding thy happy name, they weep;

The mention of thy glory is unction to the breast,
And medicine in sickness, and love and life and rest.

O one, O only mansion! O Paradise of joy!
Where tears are ever banished and smiles have no alloy,
The Lamb is all thy splendor, the Crucified thy praise;
His laud and benediction thy ransomed people raise.

Jerusalem the golden, with milk and honey blest,
Beneath thy contemplation sink heart and voice oppressed.
I know not, oh, I know not, what holy joys are there,
What radiancy of glory, what bliss beyond compare.

They stand, those halls of Zion, all jubilant with song,
And bright with many an angel, and all the martyr throng.
There is the throne of David, and there from toil released,
The shout of them that triumph, the song of them that feast.

And they who with their leader have conquered in the fight,
For ever and for ever are clad in robes of white.
Oh, land that seest no sorrow! oh, state that fear'st no strife!
Oh, royal land of flowers! oh, realm and home of life!

O sweet and blessed country, the home of God's elect!
O sweet and blessed country, that eager hearts expect!
Jesus, in mercy bring us to that dear land of rest,
Who art, with God the Father, and Spirit, ever blest.[17]

CHAPTER THIRTEEN

SIGNS AND TIMES OF THE END

Is it possible for humble and intelligent faith to forecast, at least approximately, the time of our Lord's return?

Of course, this does not mean that the Scriptures give any warrant for reckless prophesying on the part of fallible people or the making of schedules for the divine program. Our business is not to foretell the future but to study the word of prophecy that God Himself has given in the light of history and providence, God's own interpreters of His Word.

A Careful Study of the Prophetic Word

The book of Revelation encourages, by a distinct benediction, a careful study of the prophetic word, especially this particular prophetic book. After one of the most mysterious predictions, the inspired writer added, *"Here is wisdom. Let him that hath understanding count…"* (Revelation 13:18). The writer of this book was commanded not to seal the word of his prophecy, for the time was at hand. (See Revelation 22:10.) Daniel, on the contrary, was told to seal his prophecy, and he added pathetically, *"I heard, but*

I understood not." (See Daniel 12:4–13.) The light that is falling upon the prophetic page through wise and modest interpretation is one of the most remarkable signs that we are in the time of the end.

Writing to the Thessalonian Christians, the apostle Paul assured them, *"Ye, brethren, are not in darkness, that that day should overtake you as a thief.…Therefore let us not sleep, as do others; but let us watch and be sober"* (1 Thessalonians 5:4, 6). The Lord Jesus told His disciples that His coming would fall *"as a snare…on all them that dwell on the face of the whole earth"* (Luke 21:35). However, *they* were not to be surprised, but to be watching and ready so that they would escape the calamities that were to fall upon the world.

When a distinguished visitor arrives upon our shores, the announcement of his coming usually reaches the public at the time of his arrival. But to his intimate friends, his coming is known long before, and they are waiting to receive him. When the happy hour of her wedding is fixed, long before the public is aware, the bride herself knows just when it is to take place; and, indeed, she has most to say in fixing the date. It would be strange if the bride of the Lamb of God did not know at least enough of the approach of her Bridegroom to be robed and waiting. Indeed, it is in a measure true that the Lord's people have quite as much to do with hastening His coming as the Lord Himself by fulfilling the conditions and completing the preparations that He Himself has prescribed.

God's Measurement of Time

There is a most important principle that we must bear in mind in dealing with this question of the times and seasons. God does not measure time according to our calendars and chronologies, in every instance. With Him, *"one day is…as a thousand years, and a thousand years as one day"* (2 Peter 3:8). A single day is sometimes fraught with issues as momentous as those that occur in a whole century. Spiritual conditions, rather than mathematical figures, measure God's great epochs. In a very important passage, which is repeated in substance several times, it is declared that God will "[shorten] *the days*" (Mark 13:20); for *"a short work will the Lord make upon the earth"* (Romans 9:28). That is to say, just as a train sometimes accelerates its speed at the end of the schedule and makes up for lost time, so the Lord's coming will be marked by a quickened movement at the end of the age. May this perhaps be the meaning of the revised translation that some scholars have given of the Lord's last promise, *"Behold, I come quickly"* (Revelation 22:12), and make it to mean, "Behold, I come swiftly"?

Signs of the Lord's Near Return

Let us with great deference and humility attempt to trace from the Scripture itself some of the approximate signs that the Lord's coming is near at hand.

Preternatural Signs

The Lord Jesus intimated repeatedly that there would be stupendous convulsions in the natural world preceding His coming and that earth and heaven would shake with the tread of His advent march: *"There shall be…earthquakes, in divers places.…And the powers of the heavens shall be shaken"* (Matthew 24:7, 29). Such things have frequently occurred at all times in human history, but there is no doubt that they have been of singular vastness and frequency of late. The decade that has recently closed has shaken this old earth as never before; and, in three successive years, it was literally true that stupendous earthquakes followed one another in every part of the world. A moment's reflection will recall the catastrophes that visited the island of Martinique, Southern Italy and Sicily, California, Valparaiso, Northern India, Central Asia, and Japan. Truly, there were earthquakes *"in divers places."* The heavens also have not been silent in their testimony to the march of God, and there seldom has been such a time of plague, famine, and distress on the earth.

Political Signs

As we have seen, the prophet Daniel gave us a program of the political history of the nations down to the end. We have also seen that most of this has been actually fulfilled in the successive breaking up of the world's great empires and the succession of smaller kingdoms that today divide the old Roman Empire. So far as this vision is concerned, there appears to be little waiting to be fulfilled. More particularly, our Lord announced that the end would be marked by terrible wars, military armaments, and great distress in the social and political world:

> There shall be...upon the earth distress of nations, with perplexity; the sea and the waves roaring; men's hearts failing them for fear, and for looking after those things which are coming on the earth: for the powers of heaven shall be shaken.
>
> (Luke 21:25–26)

We are surely in the midst of these convulsions. The great powers of the earth are facing each other with unprecedented armaments. Recent wars have been of unusual magnitude and horror, and the future possibilities of war may well be compared, as a great soldier has already compared them, to hell. Below the surface of modern society, there are volcanic forces in the suppressed movements of socialism and anarchy that may, at any moment, overwhelm organized society and government as in the days of the French Revolution. In the commercial world, the conflict between labor and capital, and in the social world, the gulf between the masses and the classes, threaten the greatest calamities. These are ominous signs that may, at any moment, become a tragedy.

Commercial Signs

A particular indication of the time of the end is that *"many shall run to and fro, and knowledge shall be increased"* (Daniel 12:4). Was there ever such a time of running to and fro, not only on land and sea but in the very air itself? Surely, we are in the age of the steam engine, the electric motor, the wireless telegraph, the automobile, the airplane—the age of rush. And knowledge is increased. The school, the newspaper, the public library, and the printing press are scattering their leaves like the forest in autumn. Higher education is widening its circle, every branch of human knowledge is specialized, and humankind is trying its best to build a tower of Babel to reach to heaven and to fulfill the adversary's first promise, *"Ye shall be as gods"* (Genesis 3:5). A great writer has said that the nineteenth century advanced human progress more than all the centuries before it, and that the first decade of the twentieth century has surpassed the whole of the nineteenth century.

God is giving us the earnest of the coming age in the wondrous days in which we live. The progress of science may be but an introductory chapter in the advent of the millennium, an anticipation of the wider knowledge and the larger emancipation of all the powers of nature in the age to come.

Within our own time, the lightning has ceased to be destructive and has become the mightiest force in our constructive and industrial life. Every year is adding to the extraordinary discoveries of human knowledge and the forces that are being made tributary to the mind of humanity and the progress of civilization. These are but foregleams of the day when the Lord will come in person and place all these mighty agencies directly in the hands of His glorified children, giving to them a sweep of knowledge and an endowment of physical capacity that will enable them to rightly utilize these mighty forces for the high purposes of His kingdom.

Moral Signs

This is God's table of contents for the last page of human history: *"The wicked shall do wickedly: and none of the wicked shall understand"* (Daniel 12:10), and *"evil men and seducers shall wax worse and worse..."* (2 Timothy 3:13). We have only to look at the headlines of the modern newspaper to see how perfectly our age is working out this table of contents. In the United States, a distinguished Senator recently stated that 8,975 deaths from murderous assault had occurred in one year and that capital punishment had been meted out to only one hundred of the perpetrators. The statistics of divorce reveal the fact that one marriage out of every twelve in the United States ends in a family tragedy. The judges of the night courts of Chicago and New York have lately revealed an epidemic of vice and moral corruption among thousands of children in the public and even private schools between the ages of seven and twelve that rivals Sodom and Gomorrah. Conditions in England may not yet be quite so grave, but they are sufficiently alarming. France is known to be more and more given up to utter hostility to the Christian religion. Germany is rapidly coming under the influence of socialism; and rationalism has long undermined all the forces of spiritual and practical Christianity. Our age is developing original and unique types of violence and crime, and we are not far from this picture given by the Master: *"As it was in the days of* [Noah], *so shall it be also in the days of the Son of man"* (Luke 17:26).

Ecclesiastical Signs

The ecclesiastical signs include the development not only of the great apostasies that we have already described but also the conditions of declension in the Christian church, which the Lord said would mark the time of the end. What do we see today, both in the pulpit and in the pew? The loss of the old faith, the rejection of the Bible and the cross, the blotting out of the line of separation between the church and the world, the spirit of liberalism in the pulpit and the professor's chair, the spirit of worldliness and self-indulgence in the membership of most of our churches, the declining membership of the Protestant churches of Great Britain, the stationary (or almost stationary) condition in most of the churches of America, and the growth of the liquor traffic, in spite of the modern temperance crusade (to the awful extent of an increase of five gallons per head to every man, woman, and child in the United States in the past five years). These are but some of the emphatic lines that church history is writing today in fulfillment of the Master's solemn warning, *"When the Son of man cometh, shall he find faith on the earth?"* (Luke 18:8).

Spiritual Signs

The prophet Daniel also gave to us some marked spiritual indications of the last times: *"Many shall be purified, and made white, and tried; but the wicked shall do wickedly"* (Daniel 12:10). Side by side with the dark shadows would be the increasing light of faith and holiness. And so we find it true that this age of unparalleled wickedness is also an age of unequalled godliness, faith, prayer, and the outpouring of the Holy Spirit upon those who are willing to walk with God in holy obedience.

Daniel's picture indicates two stages of spiritual experience. *"Many shall be purified"* indicates what might be called the experience of personal holiness, which today is one of the marked phases of Christian life and work. The next expression, *"made white,"* denotes a deeper purity. The word *white* literally means "bright." It is the expression used in describing the Lord's transfigured glory. This denotes the special work of the Holy Spirit in preparing the Lord's hidden ones for the marriage of the Lamb. It is the wedding garment of the bride; it comes through trial and temptation victoriously overcome. Therefore, to *"made white"* is added *"and tried."*

May God help us all to be thus robed and ready for the coming of the Lord.

Jewish Signs

In a previous chapter, we referred to the remarkable providential movements of our time in connection with Israel, and the distinct fulfillment of Ezekiel's vision of the dry bones, intimating first the political restoration and later the spiritual restoration of God's chosen people. The remarkable awakening in connection with Zionism is surely a sign of the times and of the end. Only less extraordinary is the evidence of a spiritual awakening among the Jewish people and the revived interest in connection with Jewish missions and the circulation of the New Testament in Hebrew among the Jews in all countries. In addition, the attitude of foreign governments toward the Jews is a fulfillment of ancient prophecy. God said He would send *"many hunters"* and *"many fishers"* (Jeremiah 16:16) in the last days to cooperate in bringing about the Jews' return to their homeland. Surely, the Russian oppression of our time is fulfilling the former figure. The Jews are being hunted from their places of exile in these unfriendly lands, while, on the other hand, the appeal of Zionism to the national spirit suggests the fisherman drawing them back in ever-increasing numbers to the land of their fathers. The people of Israel are going home, and Christ is coming back again.

Missionary Signs

Perhaps the most significant evidence of the coming end of the present age is the intense missionary movement that is stirring the heart of every earnest section of the church today. We are in the midst of a missionary revival. And it is a new revival. Within a single generation, the great missionary enterprise has been reborn and rebaptized. All classes are being caught by this new spirit—laymen, women, businessmen, young people, and even some of those whom God has made stewards of great wealth for His cause. A new watchword has been proclaimed: the evangelization of the world in the present generation. There is a quick march today to carry the standard of the cross against the last line of the works of the enemy and to plant that standard on the strategic points of all the unoccupied fields of the world. Surely, faith can hear the undertone: *"This gospel of the kingdom shall be preached in all the world for a witness unto all nations; and then shall the end come"* (Matthew 24:14).

Chronological Signs

We have already referred to some prophetic dates in connection with the development of the nations and the great systems of evil that have been discussed in former chapters. It is proper that we should sum up the signs of the coming of the Lord Jesus by a general and fuller reference to the whole subject of prophetic times.

We have already called attention to the Year-Day Theory of prophetic time and noted that this was the principle involved in Daniel's announcement of the seventy weeks that would elapse before the coming of the Messiah. (See Daniel 9:24.) This is not the only scriptural evidence of the use of a day for a year in divine measurements of time. In the Pentateuch, we find God announcing that the period of Israel's wandering in the wilderness would be forty years, corresponding to the forty days during which the unbelieving spies had explored the land—a day for a year. (See Numbers 14:33–34.) The prophet Ezekiel was commanded to lie upon his left side and upon his right, respectively, a certain number of days, prefiguring the years of judgment that would come upon his people—a day for a year. (See Ezekiel 4:4–8.) Again, unless we have the strongest reason for a contrary interpretation in any particular passage, we are justified in adopting this standard of prophetic time.

In his scholarly volumes—*Prophetic Interpretation; The Approaching End of the Age: Viewed in the Light of History, Prophecy, and Science; Light for the Last Days; Creation Centred in Christ;* and others—the late Dr. Henry Guinness has elaborated this principle with great fullness and worked out a detailed calendar of prophetic fulfillment from the rise of the Babylonian Empire down to the present day, in which there are many striking correspondences. He has also shown by a great induction of facts and authorities how these chronological periods run parallel with great astronomical cycles. Without entering into many details, it will be sufficient here to show the fulfillment of prophetic time in connection with the various lines of prophecy embraced in the Scriptures.

The Times of the Gentiles

We have already seen that this period was to cover seven times, or 2,520 years. The question is this: When did this period begin? We must bear in mind at this point that God's great movements are gradual, both in their commencement and in their consummation. The subjugation of Israel and the supremacy of the Gentile powers did not come about in a moment of time but through forces slowly operating during many years. We may, therefore, expect that the end of Gentile rule and the restoration of Israel will come about in the same way—by gradual processes. Thus, we may expect to find several successive points of departure in our measurement, and several points of arrival corresponding. The whole process resembles a ribbon cut diagonally at both ends so that a number of lines carried horizontally from any one end to the other would be of equal length.

The earliest date of Gentile supremacy would be 747 BC, the beginning of the era of Nabonassar, king of Babylon. Twenty-five hundred and twenty years from this date brings us to the opening stages of the French Revolution, when the governments of the world received their most terrific shock, and the beginning of the end was distinctly foreshadowed. The latest period from which to begin the subjugation of Israel and the domination of the Gentiles is 587 BC, the date of the fall of Jerusalem to the Babylonians. Our measuring line from this point would bring us to the year 1933, not now far distant. Between these two periods of about a century and a half, God has certainly been working with a mighty hand in bringing about the dissolution of the great world powers that Daniel described. And before it will have expired, may we not humbly expect some glorious consummation?

Jewish Times

There are two measuring lines in connection with Israel's future. The first is 2,300 years, the date given to Daniel in the tenth chapter, measuring the oppression of his people by the eastern little horn, which represents the Islamic power. We have already seen that the starting point of this period, in all probability, was the decree of Artaxerxes for the restoration of Jerusalem in 457 BC. From this date, 2,300 years would bring us to 1844, when the Turkish government was compelled by the powers of Europe to issue a decree of toleration for both Jews and Christians. This was the beginning of a period of gradual and increasing liberty on the part of victims of Turkish oppression and the corresponding breaking down of Turkish power.

There is another date, however, given in Daniel 12:7, which is a shorter measuring line of "*a time, times, and an half*," or 1,260 years. This period, the prophet was told, was to measure the scattering of the holy people. Measuring from the year AD 637, when Jerusalem was captured by the Muslim army, 1,260 years brings us to 1897, when Zionism was organized and new forces set in motion for the final restoration of Israel, which are steadily working toward that end. At the same time, God has been moving in other providential lines, through constant revolutions in Turkey itself and the steady weakening of its power, which are cooperating by a manifest destiny to the fulfillment of His prophetic Word.

In the last chapter of Daniel, we have already seen that an extension of seventy-five years was to be added to the period already named, making in total 1,335 years. This extension would seem to embrace all the details and stages of God's final working and bring us to the end of the prophetic cycle and the glorious day of which the divine messenger declared, *"Blessed is he that waiteth, and cometh to the thousand three hundred and five and thirty days"* (Daniel 12:12).

Times of the Papacy

Again and again, both in Daniel and in Revelation, the duration of the persecuting power of the great apostasy is given as 1,260 years. Beginning our measurement with the year AD 533, when the emperor Justinian gave to the pope the decree establishing his supremacy, our measuring line would bring us exactly to 1793, the Reign of Terror and the French Revolution. This was the period when the Papacy received its first most dreadful blow, resulting, in a little while, through the wars of Napoleon, in the capture of the pope himself as a prisoner of war.

The next initial point from which we might measure the increasing dominion of Rome is the year 607. This was marked by the decree of Phocas confirming the former decree of Justinian. Again, our measuring line brings us to a still more impressive era, namely, the issuing of the decree of infallibility by the pope, followed immediately by the French and Italian wars, which ended in the final loss of the temporal power of the popes and the end of the Papacy as a world power. Since that date, it has simply been an ecclesiastical system, and never again can it claim its place among the nations.[18] There is a further date, AD 663, the decree of Vitallian. Our measuring line will bring us to a date still in the future. God has yet much to accomplish in His final dealings with this evil system. But His faithfulness in the past to the *"sure word of prophecy"* (2 Peter 1:19) encourages us to know and believe that His coming *"is near, even at the doors"* (Matthew 24:33).

When we speak of the coming of our Lord as imminent, we do not mean the fulfillment of all the successive prophecies that reach on to His glorious epiphany; there may be much to be accomplished before that day will arrive. But there is another coming for which His saints are waiting—His gracious *parousia*. It is of this that He is saying in whispered tones of warning to all His waiting ones, *"Behold, I come as a thief. Blessed is he that watcheth, and keepeth his garments…"* (Revelation 16:15).

> I know not if He come at eve,
> Or night, or morn, or noon;
> I know the breeze of twilight gray
> That fans the cheeks of dying day
> Doth ever whisper, "Soon."
>
> I know not if His chariot wheels
> Yet near or distant are;
> I only know each thunder roll
> Doth wake an echo in my soul
> That saith, "Not very far."
>
> I know not if we long must wait
> The summer of His smile;
> I only know that hope doth sweep
> With thrilling touch my heart strings deep,
> And sings, "A little while."

CHAPTER FOURTEEN

THE PRACTICAL INFLUENCE OF THE BLESSED HOPE

"And every man that hath this hope in him purifieth
himself, even as he is pure."
—1 John 3:3

What is the practical value of the blessed hope? Is it a speculation in theology, or is it a living and blessed hope and inspiration, linked in the Scriptures with almost every aspect of the Christian life?

An Incentive to the Unsaved

The apostles used this hope as an appeal to the careless and indifferent to urge them to make a decision for Christ.

Repent ye therefore, and be converted, that your sins may be blotted out, when the times of refreshing shall come from the

presence of the Lord; and he shall send Jesus Christ, which
before was preached unto you: whom the heavens must receive
until the times of restitution of all things.   (Acts 3:19–21)

And again, Paul spoke of the Thessalonians as having "*turned*
to God from idols to serve the living and true God; and to wait for his
Son from heaven, whom he raised from the dead, even Jesus, which
delivered us from the wrath to come" (1 Thessalonians 1:9–10).

Therefore, it must have been presented to them as a practical incentive and a message of warning. We should use this message of awakening and conviction more freely and effectually than
we do. It was the message of God's coming judgment that led to
Nineveh's repentance (see Jonah 3), and the proclamation to the
heathen of Christ's coming has brought many to bow at the feet
of Jesus.

A Motive for Personal Holiness

Thus the apostle Paul taught in his letter to Titus:

The grace of God that bringeth salvation hath appeared to all
men, teaching us that, denying ungodliness and worldly lusts,
we should live soberly, righteously, and godly, in this present
world; looking for that blessed hope, and the glorious appear-
ing of the great God and our Saviour Jesus Christ; who gave
himself for us, that he might redeem us from all iniquity, and
purify unto himself a peculiar people, zealous of good works.
(Titus 2:11–14)

And again, in writing to the Thessalonians, Paul presented the
coming of the Lord as the great goal of holy aspiration: "*The very*
God of peace sanctify you wholly; and I pray God your whole spirit and
soul and body be preserved blameless unto the coming of our Lord Jesus
Christ" (1 Thessalonians 5:23).

The beloved John likewise linked this hope with the practice of holiness: "*When he shall appear, we shall be like him; for we shall see him as he is. And every man that hath this hope in him purifieth himself, even as he is pure*" (1 John 3:2–3). Because we are going to be like Him then, we wear His image now. We anticipate our coming glory; and, like the Lord Himself, who began to wear the garments of His incarnation long before He came to earth, so we try on, even here, the robes of our approaching coronation. The glory of the Holiest shone through the curtains, and so the glory of our future state should cover us even here.

This is our special preparation for His coming, and such a preparation on the part of His church is the most marked sign of His advent. When you see the bride arrayed in her wedding robes, you know the Bridegroom must be near. And if we could see the church of Christ robed in the beauty of holiness and putting on her wedding garments, we would know that day was near, and that the angel voices were about to proclaim, "*The marriage of the Lamb is come, and his wife hath made herself ready*" (Revelation 19:7).

An Incentive to Heavenly-Mindedness

In her wonderful little tract "He Is Coming Tomorrow," Mrs. Stowe has pictured the consternation of a millionaire and the consolation of a poor suffering child of God at the announcement that had just been made to the waiting ones: "He is coming tomorrow." This was what Paul meant when he said to the Philippians,

For our citizenship is in the heavens, whence also a Saviour we await—the Lord Jesus Christ—who shall transform the body of our humiliation to its becoming conformed to the body of his glory. (Philippians 3:20–21 YLT)

There is nothing except the love of Jesus that can so separate us from the world as the hope of Christ's coming. Dr. Chalmers describes the inhabitants of a pestilential marsh who had again and again been urged to emigrate, but they could not be induced to leave the certainty of their life in the marsh for an uncertain good. At last, one day, they saw approaching and slowly passing by a beauteous isle, clothed with a verdure and loveliness they had never seen before and breathing the balmy air of its glad and eternal spring over all their unhealthy plains.

Then they began to eagerly inquire if they might enter its blessed harbor. They sent out their boats across the sea, entreated permission to land upon its shores, and gladly let go of their old cabins and treasures and hastened to the happy shores of this bright and holy paradise. So is the vision of the coming of the Lord Jesus. It falls like a withering spell on earthly ambition and avarice, and makes us cry,

> My hopes are passing upward, onward,
> And with my hopes my heart has gone;
> My eyes are turning skyward, sunward,
> Where glory brightens round yon throne.[19]

It Keeps Us Close to Him

> *And now, little children, abide in him; that, when he shall appear, we may have confidence, and not be ashamed before him at his coming.* (1 John 2:28)

When Elisha knew that Elijah's translation was near, he kept very close to his side. To every suggestion that he should leave his side, he answered, "*As the* LORD *liveth, and as thy soul liveth, I will not leave thee*" (2 Kings 2:2, 4, 6). So, if we are waiting and watching for His coming, we will not let a moment separate us from Him. It was but one evening that Thomas was absent, but that very evening, Jesus came. (See John 20:19–24.)

An Incentive to Brotherly Love

The Lord make you to increase and abound in love one toward another, and toward all men, even as we do toward you: to the end he may stablish your hearts unblameable in holiness before God, even our Father, at the coming of our Lord Jesus Christ with all his saints.   (1 Thessalonians 3:12–13)

How embarrassing it would be for you and your brother to meet tomorrow at His right hand, and, looking in His face, to say, "Lord, I do not speak to him." A day is coming when we will all clasp hands and look into each other's eyes, and say, "Well, we did not understand each other, but it is all right at last." Why not assume that we may be mistaken, and love even His erring children for His sake?

A Call to Vigilance

Watch therefore, for ye know neither the day nor the hour wherein the Son of man cometh.   (Matthew 25:13)

Let your loins be girded about, and your lights burning; and ye yourselves like unto men that wait for their lord, when he will return from the wedding; that when he cometh and knocketh, they may open unto him immediately. Blessed are those servants, whom the lord when he cometh shall find watching: verily I say unto you, that he shall gird himself, and make them to sit down to meat, and will come forth and serve them. And if he shall come in the second watch, or come in the third watch, and find them so, blessed are those servants. And this know, that if the goodman of the house had known what hour the thief would come, he would have watched, and not have suffered his house to be broken through. Be ye therefore ready

*also: for the Son of man cometh at an hour when ye think
not.* (Luke 12:35–40)

Here are two ways of receiving the Master. One is to "*open
unto him immediately.*" The other is to allow His house "*to be broken
through.*" Which will we have? Purposely, the time of His coming
is unknown so that we may be ever ready, but we know enough to
recognize that it is near.

The late Dr. A. J. Gordon once sent word to his family in the
country that he was coming to them some day the following week.
Every evening, his little children washed, dressed, and went down to
meet the one suburban train that came to the village, in order to welcome him. He did not come till Saturday, but his wife told him that
the hope of his coming had kept the children in clean garments the
whole week. So may this blessed hope purify us "*even as he is pure.*"

Patience in view of His Coming

*Be patient, therefore, brethren, unto the coming of the Lord.
Behold, the husbandman waiteth for the precious fruit of the
earth, and hath long patience for it, until he receive the early
and latter rain. Be ye also patient; stablish your hearts: for the
coming of the Lord draweth nigh.* (James 5:7–8)

"*Let your moderation be known unto all men. The Lord is at hand.
Be careful* ["*anxious*" NKJV, YLT] *for nothing…*" (Philippians 4:5–6).
Those whose hopes are above the world are not greatly tried by its
passing clouds. Oh, how easy it will make our little worries, frets,
and conflicts when we truly realize

A few more struggles here,
A few more partings o'er,
A few more toils, a few more tears,
And we shall weep no more.[20]

An Encouragement to Steadfastness

> Be ye stedfast, unmoveable, always abounding in the work of
> the Lord, forasmuch as ye know that your labour is not in vain
> in the Lord.   (1 Corinthians 15:58)

> Cast not away therefore your confidence, which hath great rec-
> ompense of reward....For yet a little while, and he that shall
> come will come, and will not tarry.   (Hebrews 10:35, 37)

Hold on—the end is near; the reward is great. Too much
has already been suffered to lose the victory now. *"Hold that fast
which thou hast, that no man take thy crown"* (Revelation 3:11).
Standing on yonder battlements, He holds the crown in view.
You can almost hear the plaudits and the shouts. Will you falter
now?

An Inspiration in Our Work

*"Behold, I come quickly; and my reward is with me, to give every
man according as his work shall be"* (Revelation 22:12). And so to
the humble reaper, to the faithful pastor, to the soul-winning
evangelist, the New Testament holds out evermore this great
hope as an inspiration and recompense. How ashamed some
of us would feel if we received a crown! We would almost walk
through the palaces of glory as if we had stolen it! Not so Paul.
He will know the name of every jewel in his diadem. There is
Lydia. There is Timothy. There is the Philippian jailor. There
is Sosthenes, who attacked him at Corinth and was subsequently saved in glorious "revenge." There is the soldier who
was chained to his side. Are you forging your crown and gathering its jewels, or will you be *"ashamed before him at his coming"*
(1 John 2:28)?

Consolation in Sorrow

I would not have you to be ignorant, brethren, concerning them which are asleep, that ye sorrow not, even as others which have no hope....For the Lord himself shall descend from heaven with a shout, with the voice of the archangel, and with the trump of God: and the dead in Christ shall rise first: then we which are alive and remain shall be caught up together with them in the clouds ["in clouds" YLT], to meet the Lord in the air: and so shall we ever be with the Lord. Wherefore comfort one another with these words.

(1 Thessalonians 4:13, 16–18)

This doctrine is the balm for sorrow and the comfort for bereavement. It gives us back, in immortal beauty and everlasting love, those whom we have lost, and it wipes away every tear. *"Be ye stedfast, unmoveable, always abounding in the work of the Lord, forasmuch as ye know that your labour is not in vain in the Lord"* (1 Corinthians 15:58).

There shall be no more crying,
There shall be no more pain,
There shall be no more dying,
There shall be no more stain.

Hearts that by death were riven
Meet in eternal love;
Lives on the altar given
Rise to their crowns above.

Jesus is coming surely,
Jesus is coming soon;
Oh, let us walk so purely,
Oh, let us keep our crown!

CHAPTER FIFTEEN

THE LORD'S COMING AND MISSIONS

"This gospel of the kingdom shall be preached in all the world for a witness unto all nations; and then shall the end come."
—Matthew 24:14

"And I saw another angel fly in the midst of heaven, having the everlasting gospel to preach unto them that dwell on the earth, and to every nation, and kindred, and tongue, and people, saying with a loud voice, Fear God, and give glory to him; for the hour of his judgment is come."
—Revelation 14:6–7

The coming of Christ is the great end of creation and redemption. It is the day for which all other days were made, the one event to which all other things are tending.

Even nature itself foreshadows the new creation. This fallen world, with its minor key of sadness, echoes in every tone the cry for something better than nature knows. *"The whole creation groaneth and travaileth in pain together…waiting for the adoption, to wit, the redemption of* [the] *body"* (Romans 8:22–23). Every radiant morning, every returning spring, every bursting bud and breathing blossom, and every humming insect emerging from its wintry tomb and opening chrysalis is but the prophecy of the resurrection and our re-creation, when the One who sits upon the throne will say, *"Behold, I make all things new"* (Revelation 21:5).

Something Better than this World

Man's highest philanthropy aims to develop and improve the conditions of this old earth of ours so that, someday, it will fulfill the dreams of that golden age of which poets have sung. But it would be a poor reflection upon God if this old world at its best was the highest that His power and goodness could achieve for the human race. When we think of the ravages of sickness, sin, and sorrow; when we realize the malign elements in the earthquake, the tempest, and the devouring sea; and when we look at the moldering dust and the hopelessness and agony of death; and we remember that, after all, the fairest scenes of earth are but cemeteries and the spots that tell of broken hearts and blighted hopes, well may we say,

> Were this poor world our only rest,
> Living or dying, none were blessed.

Or, as the apostle Paul has expressed it, *"If in this life only we have hope in Christ, we are of all men most miserable"* (1 Corinthians 15:19).

No, God's wisdom and love have something better for our race than civilization, reformation, social reform, and scientific progress; something better even than a spiritual millennium and the worldwide triumph of the gospel and the grace of God.

Just as, for the individual, God's highest thought is not self-improvement or the best possible result out of natural character and human culture but a new creation—a regeneration so complete that old things pass away and all things are made new—so, too, for the world itself, God's plan is the same. The mark of the cross must pass upon the earth itself, and, through death and resurrection, it must come forth as a new earth to take its place with God's new heavens in the coming age. The city of God does not spring up from the earth; as the New Jerusalem, it comes down from heaven. Jesus Christ is the *"nobleman* [who] *went into a far country to receive for himself a kingdom, and to return"* (Luke 19:12). Ages have passed since He went away, and, from generation to generation, He has been gathering the stones for that glorious city that, in a little while, will burst from the heavens upon an astonished world and take the place of all our puny structures and all our petty plans.

This was the vision of the ancient prophets; this was the promise of the departing Lord; and this is the great perspective that climaxes the vision of faith and hope throughout the whole New Testament.

Something Better than an Earthly Millennium

For too long, the church of God has closed the vision with the establishment of the church and the conversion of the world as the real end for which the Spirit is working in this age. But, if we look at the inspired record, we find that there is yet another scene in the picture that lifts our thoughts to a higher plane and a more distant horizon. It begins in Acts 1, where two men in white apparel stood by Jesus' disciples, saying, *"Ye men of Galilee, why stand ye gazing up into heaven? this same Jesus, which is taken up from you into heaven, shall so come in like manner as ye have seen him go into heaven"* (Acts 1:11).

Ah, this was needed to complete the perspective. Away beyond the church, the mission field, and the present age stretched the vista of millennial years, with the glorious light of the Lord's return as the real goal toward which redemption is ever moving forward and the Holy Spirit is ever leading on. Until we get this picture fully in view, we have not grasped God's great plan, we have not gotten our eye on the true goal, and our course will be unsteady and our work unbalanced.   .

The Hope of the Early Church

It was for this that the apostolic church was ever watching, praying, working, and waiting. This was the message that the apostle Paul preached to the Thessalonians, which made them "[turn] *to God from idols to serve the living and true God; and to wait for his Son from heaven*" (1 Thessalonians 1:9–10). This was the comfort Paul held out to the bereaved and sorrowing saints as they bid farewell to the martyred forms of their beloved ones—that Christ was coming soon, and they would be *"caught up together with them... to meet the Lord in the air"* (1 Thessalonians 4:17). This was the joy and crown of his own intense ministry, that he might present his people to the heavenly Bridegroom in the day of His coming as his *"crown of rejoicing...in the presence of our Lord Jesus Christ at his coming"* (1 Thessalonians 2:19). And this was his own inspiring hope as he was about to lay down his ministry and meet his Lord: *"Henceforth there is laid up for me a crown of righteousness, which the Lord, the righteous judge, shall give me at that day"* (2 Timothy 4:8).

The Plan of God

When the apostles were starting out on the great task of the world's evangelization, a great council was held in Jerusalem to settle certain principles for the guidance of the church of the present age. And to that council, the Holy Spirit revealed through its leader, the apostle James, as he quoted from the ancient prophet Amos, the divine order of events in the program of the Lord. The first of these steps was stated thus: *"God at the first did visit the Gentiles, to take out of them a people for his name"* (Acts 15:14). The second stage was as definitely stated in the next part: *"After this [God] will return, and will build again the tabernacle of David, which is fallen down"* (Acts 15:16). Here we find the Lord's coming presented as the sequel to their immediate ministry, the great event for which they were gathering out a people from the Gentile nations.

If the church had always kept this purpose in view, she would have saved herself the waste of much vain effort and bitter disappointment in her attempts to build up a permanent earthly institution and to create on earth a kingdom without the King. For the church itself has been as much at fault in her objects and ambitions as the world has in its mere human policy.

People have tried to establish their cities and kingdoms as if they would reign forever, and to make this earth a paradise of pleasure without the Lord. And sin has cursed all their ambitions and policies and turned the vision of earthly pride and power into that fearful menagerie of wild beasts that Daniel saw when he looked at the governments of earth as they appeared in the light of heaven. But just as foolish and shortsighted is the policy of the Christian worker who aims to establish, even through the church, an earthly millennium.

The City of the Living God

Earth offers no foundation stable enough for *"the city of the living God, the heavenly Jerusalem"* (Hebrews 12:22). Our business is to gather stones, timbers, and jewels for that glorious edifice and to pass them on to the great Architect who is building, over yonder, the *"city which hath foundations"* (Hebrews 11:10) and the *"kingdom which cannot be moved"* (Hebrews 12:28).

We are just like Hiram's carpenters and Solomon's stonecutters, working in the mountains of Lebanon and the quarries of Judah and passing the cedar and the granite to its future site. One by one, we are gathering the souls that He is fitting into the living temple; and, in a little while, the vision of its glory will burst upon our view, and admiring angels will say, "Come and see the bride, the Lamb's wife." (See Revelation 21:9.) And we will behold *"that great city, the holy Jerusalem, descending out of heaven from God, having the glory of God: and…light…like unto a stone most precious, even like a jasper stone, clear as crystal"* (Revelation 21:10–11).

> *And the twelve gates were twelve pearls:…and the street of the city was pure gold, as it were transparent glass.…And the city had no need of the sun, neither of the moon, to shine in it: for the glory of God did lighten it, and the Lamb is the light thereof. And the nations of them which are saved shall walk in the light of it: and the kings of the earth do bring their glory and honour into it.* (Revelation 21:21, 23–24)

The True Goal

This is the glorious goal. This is the future toward which the cross of Calvary and the Holy Spirit are leading the generations. This is the true end for which it is worth our while to work and pray. This is the transcendent outlook of faith and hope and love. This is the kingdom that Daniel saw, superseding the pride and power of Babylon, Persia, Greece, and Rome, when

> *the kingdom and dominion, and the greatness of the kingdom under the whole heaven, shall be given to the people of the saints of the most High, whose kingdom is an everlasting*

kingdom, and all dominions shall serve and obey him.

(Daniel 7:27)

This is the glorious consummation that the *"great voices in heaven"* celebrate in Revelation 11 when they cry,

The kingdoms of this world are become the kingdoms of our Lord, and of his Christ; and he shall reign for ever and ever.... [The twenty-four elders say,] *We give thee thanks, O LORD God Almighty, which art, and wast, and art to come; because thou hast taken to thee thy great power, and hast reigned.*

(Revelation 11:15, 17)

This is what the Master meant when He said, *"And when these things begin to come to pass, then look up* ["bend yourselves back" YLT], *and lift up your heads; for your redemption draweth nigh"* (Luke 21:28).

The Gospel of the Kingdom

The work of missions is the great means of hastening that end. The work of the Holy Spirit through the church was chiefly intended to gather out from all nations a people for His name, a bride for the Lamb. At the present time, it is not God's purpose to bring people to the acceptance of Christ as their Savior and King by any stronger compulsion than the persuasion of the gospel and the influence of the Holy Spirit. In the next age, every knee will bow and every tongue confess that He is Lord (see Philippians 2:10–11), but at the present time, the gospel is preached to people as a witness. The opportunity is given to everyone, and then it is left to their voluntary choice. *"He that believeth and is baptized shall be saved; but he that believeth not shall be damned"* (Mark 16:16).

The purpose of the present dispensation is to give this universal probation for a brief time to all the races of humankind. After the opportunity has been given, and all who are willing to come to Him have accepted the gracious invitation, God will close the day of grace and bring the nations before Him in judgment. Then He will establish a visible kingdom on earth that will compel the subjection of all humankind and bring earth's millions, without exception, to bow to His scepter.

Today, it is the few that He is calling—not the subjects of the coming age but the rulers of it. Just as David called out the heroes who followed him in the days of his exile, and afterward made them the princes of his kingdom, so the Lord Jesus today is training the men and women who will share with Him the government of the age to come. This is our high honor and privilege: to be kings and priests unto God and to reign with Him upon the earth. (See Revelation 5:10.)

His Coming Delayed

Until the whole number of God's elect will have been thus called and gathered home, the coming of the Lord Jesus would seem to be delayed. This elect company is universal in its scope, while limited in its numbers. It embraces the people of every land, tribe, and tongue. The angel of the Apocalypse had the *"everlasting gospel to preach unto…every nation, and kindred, and tongue, and people"* (Revelation 14:6). Therefore, today, the work of missions must be worldwide. It is not enough for us to be zealous in gathering a large number of converts among a favored people in Christian lands. God wants us to bring the representatives of earthly tongues, and when this has been done, then, He tells us, the end will come. The bride of the Lamb, like the Son of Man, must represent humanity as a whole. The Lord Jesus is not a Jew, an Anglo-Saxon, or a Greek but the Son of Man, the representative of every race—universal man. Accordingly, His bride must be the daughter of humanity, the composite photograph, embracing every feature, every color, and every kindred of the human family.

The Lamb's Bride

It is said that when a great artist was asked to paint the empress of Russia, he traveled all over the country and sought opportunity to see every beautiful woman of the land. Then, in his painting, he combined the most beautiful feature or expression in each of these faces into one composite picture—taking care, of course, to make the countenance of the empress the most distinctive of all. And then he presented it to her with incomparable flattery as her portrait. The heavenly Artist is not painting, but creating, a bride characterized by all that is most distinctive of every type of redeemed humanity—all, together, reflecting the matchless glory and beauty of the Lord Jesus Himself.

All Nations

Consequently, the work of missions must be universal. Thank God that the great ideal is being rapidly fulfilled. Already, more than four hundred of the languages of earth have repeated the story of the Savior's love, and all the forces of divine providence and grace are working as never before to prepare the world for the entrance of the gospel and to gather out of the nations *"a people for [God's] name"* (Acts 15:14).

How manifestly His arm has been made bare (see Isaiah 52:10) in the breaking down of the Roman Catholic and Muslim barriers in Turkey, France, Italy, Spain, the Philippines, the West Indies, and the South American republics. How He has used the ambitions of European colonizing governments to open the interior of Africa and has sent the explorer and the promoter to lead the way for the missionary. How the steamship, the railroad, the postal union, and the foreign consul in China, India, and Africa have become the handmaidens of the gospel. What a romance of missions the story of the progress of Japan, Siam [Thailand], China, and Korea has been for a quarter of a century. How fully God has answered the prayers of His people a generation ago and opened all the doors of long-closed lands. And how marvelously the Holy Spirit has been seconding the providence of God and pouring out a great missionary spirit in almost every heathen land.

Truly, one is reminded of the message that came to a Christian worker recently in a dream. He saw a great battlefield and thousands of horses, all caparisoned and ready to charge. But there were no riders, and when he asked someone standing by for an explanation, this was the answer: "These horses are God's great missionary opportunities today." But where are the riders? Where are the people to enter God's open doors? Where?

Surely, the message that came to David at Baal Perazim may well ring in our ears today: *"And let it be, when thou hearest the sound of a going in the tops of the mulberry trees, that then thou shalt bestir thyself: for then shall the* LORD *go out before thee, to smite the host of the Philistines"* (2 Samuel 5:24).

> There's a sound of a going in the air
> That is more than the whispering Zephyr's sigh;
> There's a sound in the tops of the mulberry trees
> That tells us the hosts of the Lord are nigh.
>
> For the Ancient of Days is on His way,
> And the hour of His judgment is at hand,
> And the shaking of heaven and earth today
> Is troubling every wondering land.
>
> We are going forth to a strenuous fight,
> To a sword of fire and a field of blood,

> To the slums of sin and the lands of night,
> And the last stern battle of the Lord.
>
> Let us gird ourselves for the glorious fray,
> Let us stir ourselves till the fight be won,
> For the Son of God is on His way,
> And the Lord of Hosts is leading on.[21]

How vain and fruitless are all our efforts to help humanity and reform society short of God's plan! Are we wasting our strength in second-class philanthropies and enterprises? They are not worth the cost. The time is too short; the crisis is too near; the conditions are too hard. Nothing else will help our ruined world but Christ, His cross, and His coming. Do not sink your money in the sands of time, but put all the strength of your life into the best things, the one thing—the only thing that God has given us as the remedy for sin and the business of life.

How unsatisfactory are many of the religious methods and movements of our time! How poorly spent the money that you put into a church choir, a splendid organ, a church spire, and an institutional church that is little better than a Sunday club and a place of more respectable amusement for so-called Christians. How needless are even costly missionary institutions for a world that will soon hear the thunders of His voice. More simply, more swiftly, let us fly, like the angel of the Apocalypse, with the everlasting gospel to preach to every kindred, tribe, and tongue.

Let us be wise to understand our Master's plan! Let us be swift to hear His voice and to obey His command! Let us make sure of that glorious reward. "*They that turn many to righteousness* [will shine] *as the stars for ever and ever*" (Daniel 12:3). Let everyone have some part in this magnificent crusade. If you cannot go, you can send. Your prayers can be eloquent; your gifts and sacrifices can give you a substitute and an equal place in the army roll and the glorious recompense.

Come away from the vain and perishing things of time, from the mistaken though well-meant enterprises of humanitarian zeal and from the selfishness and sin of a fruitless and wasted Christian life. Invest the strength of your being in the greatest work in the world, the *"city which hath foundations, whose builder and maker is God"* (Hebrews 11:10) and the *"kingdom which cannot be moved"* (Hebrews 12:28).

> The Master's coming draweth near,
> The Son of man will soon appear,
> His kingdom is at hand.
> But ere that glorious day can be,
> This Gospel of the Kingdom we
> Must preach in every land.
>
> Oh, let us then His coming haste,
> Oh, let us end this awful waste
> Of souls that never die.
> A thousand millions still are lost,
> A Saviour's blood has paid the cost,
> Oh, hear their dying cry!
>
> They're passing, passing fast away,
> A hundred thousand souls a day,
> In Christless guilt and gloom.
> Oh, Church of Christ, what wilt thou say
> When in the awful judgment day
> They charge thee with their doom?[22]

NOTES

1. *Premillennialism* is defined as "the view that Christ's return will usher in a future millennium of Messianic rule [on earth]." *Postmillennialism* is defined as "the theological doctrine that the second coming of Christ will occur after the millennium." See *Merriam-Webster's 11ᵗʰ Collegiate Dictionary*, electronic version, © 2003, s.v. *premillennialism, postmillennialism*.
2. Dr. and Mrs. H. Grattan Guinness, *Light for the Last Days: A Study in Chronological Prophecy* (1888), chapter 7. See http://www.historicism.com/Guinness/Light/light7.htm.
3. Lord Byron, "Oh! Weep for Those," *Original Hebrew Melodies* (1815).
4. Omar, also called Umar, was the second Muslim caliph, or ruler, after the death of Muhammad; it was to him that Sophronius surrendered the city of Jerusalem in AD 637 after it was besieged by Omar's army.
5. Henry Grattan Guinness, *History Unveiling Prophecy; or, Time as an Interpreter* (New York: Fleming H. Revell Co., 1905), 391–392.
6. Editor's note: The material in the italicized brackets was included by Young; the material in Roman brackets was added for clarity.

7. Edward Gibbon, *Decline and Fall of the Roman Empire, Vol. 4* (1788), http://www.sacred-texts.com/cla/gibbon/04/daf04032.htm.

8. Roman Catholic writer Augustine Steuchus, quoted in Albert Barnes, *Notes, Explanatory and Practical, on the Book of Revelation* (New York: Harper & Brothers, Publishers, 1852), 421.

9. "The whole world is her seat."

10. Frankish ruler, and grandfather of Charlemagne.

11. Thomas Moore.

12. Horatius Bonar, "A Stranger Here," 1857.

13. Andrew Bonar.

14. A mandarin is "a public official in the Chinese Empire of any of nine superior grades," *Merriam-Webster's 11ᵗʰ Collegiate Dictionary*, electronic version, © 2003, s.v. *mandarin*, 1a.

15. Henry Wadsworth Longfellow, "The Arsenal at Springfield" (1845).

16. A. B. Simpson, "Some Sweet Morn," 1897.

17. Bernard of Cluny, excerpts from his poem "On the Contempt of the World," circa 1140, from which the hymns "For Thee, O Dear, Dear Country" and "Jerusalem the Golden" were derived.

18. Vatican City was recognized by Italy as an independent city-state in 1929 by the Lateran Treaty.

19. Horatius Bonar, "A Stranger Here."

20. Horatius Bonar, "A Few More Years Shall Roll."

21. A. B. Simpson, "A Sound in the Mulberry Trees."

22. A. B. Simpson, "A Missionary Cry."

ABOUT THE AUTHOR

Albert Benjamin Simpson (1843–1919) was born to parents of Scottish descent and grew to become one of the most respected Christian figures in American evangelicalism. A much-sought-after speaker and pastor, Simpson founded a major evangelical denomination, published more than seventy books, edited a weekly magazine for nearly forty years, and wrote many gospel songs and poems.

The first few years of his life were spent in relative simplicity on Prince Edward Island, Canada, where his father, an elder in the Presbyterian church, worked as a shipbuilder and eventually became involved in the export/import industry. To avoid an approaching business depression, the family moved to Ontario, where the younger Simpson accepted Christ as his Savior at age fifteen and was subsequently "called by God to preach" the gospel of Christ.

Simpson went on to pastor New York's 13th Street Presbyterian Church. However, in 1881, he resigned and began to hold independent evangelistic meetings in New York City. A year later, the Gospel Tabernacle was built, and Simpson began to turn his vision toward establishing an organization for missions.

Simpson helped to form and lead two evangelization societies: The Christian Alliance and The Evangelical Missionary Alliance. As thousands joined these two groups, Simpson sensed a need for the two to become one. In 1897, they became The Christian and Missionary Alliance.

Paul Rader, former pastor of the Moody Church in Chicago, once said, "[Simpson] was the greatest heart preacher I ever listened to. He preached out of his own rich dealings with God."

On October 28, 1919, Simpson slipped into a coma from which he never recovered. Family members recall that his final words were spoken to God in prayer for all the missionaries he had helped to send throughout the world.

Welcome to Our House!

We Have a Special Gift for You ...

It is our privilege and pleasure to share in your love of Christian classics by publishing books that enrich your life and encourage your faith.

To show our appreciation, we invite you to sign up to receive a specially selected **Reader Appreciation Gift**, with our compliments. Just go to the Web address at the bottom of this page.

God bless you as you seek a deeper walk with Him!

WE HAVE A GIFT FOR YOU

whpub.me/classicthx

WHITAKER
HOUSE